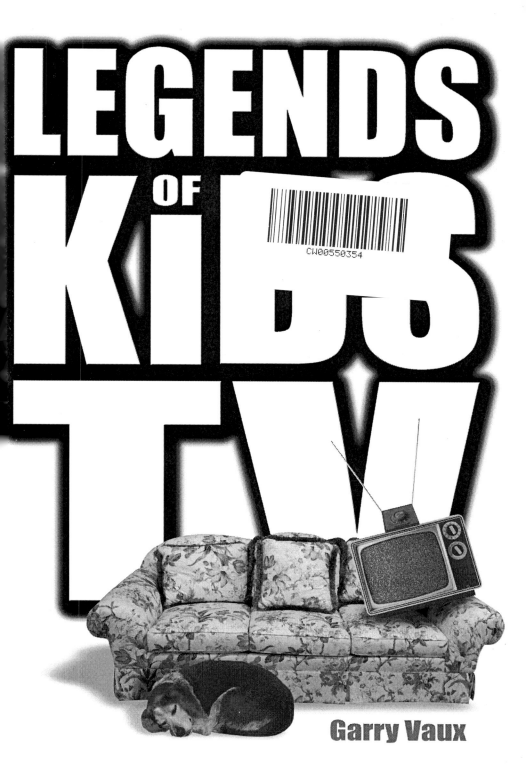

LEGENDS
OF
KiDS TV

Garry Vaux

Published in Great Britain by

GJB Publishing
Studio 1, 115 Molesey Avenue,
West Molesey, Surrey KT8 2ES
www.GJBpublishing.co.uk

Printed in Great Britain by

Ridgeway Press Limited
12 Campbell Court, Bramley,
Tadley, Hampshire RG26 5EG

with thanks to:

Willy Finlayson, Paul Abbott, John Garner,
Trish & Ray Bignall, Rick Jones, Bob Noble, Angus Auden
and Jerk City, 189 Wardour Street, London

This book was conceived, created, designed, typeset and
compiled by Garry Vaux, so please look after it!

Who is Victor Grimble?

To mum.
Thank you for everything – always.

CONTENTS

FOREWORD

There was a program called 'Let's Pretend', and it aired every Saturday morning on CBS radio. My mother, my Gran my sister and I, and sometimes, even my Dad would gather 'round the old mahogany Phillips radio with the filigreed grill and green glowing dial, and be transported to the ancient Middle East, where Sultans plotted and heroes on white horses raced through the desert to save a Princess, or, perhaps the locale would be nowhere in particular; Fairyland, or an unnamed European fastness, where demons roamed and witches weaved scary spells. A kid was forced to imagine the scene, and we did, swirling through our own Tim Burton inner landscapes. We didn't have television then — oh, it existed, but it was still an alien technology in rural Canada — and I often wondered if perhaps children of the Television Age had been disenfranchised somehow, precluded from this auditory magic carpet, and stuck in the world of concrete images.

But one evening after work, when I was living in London, I walked past our sitting room and saw my two daughters silent and rapt as I had been listening to 'Let's Pretend', as something called Zebedee boinked about and an odd long-haired dog swept the floor. It was obvious that their minds were engaged — they took no notice of me — and I realised then that every generation has it's own 'Let's Pretend', and they were as 'transported' as I had been. I feel very lucky to have been an agent of this magic.

Rick Jones
Fingerbobs

INTRODUCTION

My mum passed away in 2004. It was a devastating experience and since then, it felt more and more like the last links to my childhood had been broken. It made me reflect on my childhood days in Yorkshire and all the elements that made up those times; Beano Books at Christmas, my yellow go-cart, toy cars kept in a suitcase, caravan holidays by the coast, my Spectrum 48K, a menagerie of pets, drawing cartoons, making models from cereal boxes and hours glued to the box. My mum warned me that my eyes would go square – and they did!

Bagpuss, Doctor Who, Grange Hill, The Adventure Game, Fingerbobs, Rainbow, Pogles Wood, Crackerjack, Swap Shop (to name but a few) were all an integral part of my childhood and I began to wonder what happened to the people who had entertained me so much and what they were doing now. Some people were harder to track down than others, but all the more satisfying when I did finally get in touch with them. I have the internet to thank for this as it's been an invaluable resource, without which this book would have been considerably thinner!

I originally started researching this book back in 2005 and I've been compiling it on and off since then. My mum always used to say I was a bit of a two-minute wonder and she was so right! But since her passing I developed a new-found determination to actually finish something I'd started, and so here we are – a unique collection of interviews with the stars themselves – a very bitter-sweet project, personally, but one which has created some new friendships, and something I'm sure she would be proud of.

I've included several of my own favourites, and, as not everyone is a child of the 70's, I've incorporated different eras to my own as everyone will have their own personal legends. It has brought back so many happy memories and I hope it will help you relive your childhood and give you as big a thrill as it did me, after all I am just a big kid at heart.

Aren't we all?

Garry Vaux

TONI ARTHUR
PLAY SCHOOL, PLAYAWAY

I was always fascinated by Toni Arthur. This bohemian looking woman with such a male-sounding name had me perplexed for years. But Toni was also so multi-faceted, an accomplished singer and musician and always so full of energy and enthusiasm, and anyone who can perform "The Court of King Caractacus" with all the actions and no mistakes is worthy of legendary status for that alone. Toni tells how her career has taken her around the world several times over and how a piece of artwork caused an embarrassing encounter with George Melly!

"I was singing in a folk club (I did this for a living for a while and made loads of records. This was with my first husband and we were called Dave and Toni Arthur. It was all very traditional English folk music and a lot of it was unaccompanied. If I listen to it now I cringe. For some reason all of us at the time sang with this sort of countryfied accent. We travelled all over the world doing tours - America, USSR, Africa etc. All long hair and hippy dress) and BBC producer, Peter Charlton was in the audience. At that time Dave played the guitar but always took seemingly twenty years between songs to retune.

So I gabbled away and was in serious danger of almost becoming a stand-up comedian before it's time. Peter liked this and the singing so asked me to audition for *Play School*. I'd never heard of it, but looked at the script they sent me, and having attended the Stanislavsky School of Drama in London for some terms, I decided to give it a go. I remember wearing a pink sort of shirt dress that came down to the bottom of my knickers and long pink suede boots that came up over my knees. They asked me to look at the playback of my audition and as my first reaction was "Jesus! What do I look like? That's not a children's presenter!!" they took me on! *Playaway* was to start only a few months afterwards and this was a try out for that really. They were looking for more of an entertainer and I fitted the bill, I suppose, because I became the regular girl on that only a little while afterwards.

Before this I was a precocious little sod! My parents were just lovely but we were a bit poor. Dad was a milkman and mum was a school secretary. I turned out to be quite bright, so they said, and they encouraged me all the way.

I won a music scholarship at the age of 9 to the Royal Academy of Music for piano and singing and then got a special academic scholarship to the Mary Datchelor Girls' School which specialised in music and arts. The teachers

came there from Royal Academy which saved a lot of travel. I won prizes there for drama and speech, but I took sciences at 'A' Level as I didn't have too good a literature background.

After school I went to University College Hospital to study nursing and Friern Barnet to study mental nursing and after that I went to UCL to study psychology.

I went on to marry a folk singer and gave everything up to travel the world, sing and play folk music and have two sons – Jay and Tim. I also wrote books and plays which have all been published.

Amongst the shows I appeared in as a kids presenter include *Play School*, *Playaway*, *Seeing and Doing*, *Watch* and my own series *Take a Ticket to.....* and also appeared on *Good Morning Britain*, *Woman's Hour* as well as numerous magazine programmes.

I've got quite a varied CV. After my stint on TV I ran a drama school for 7 years in Tunbridge Wells. (with some very famous ex-pupils) and was artistic director of two youth theatres. I also became a Speaker Trainer for various corporate companies which I have done all over the world.

After I divorced I went back to university to take another degree in "The use and misuse of community drama" and ended up marrying my tutor Malcolm Hay who was also the Comedy Editor for *Time Out* magazine at the time, and from this I've started directing stand-up comedians for their Edinburgh shows. I still do this. I had 6 shows up there in 2008 and I've been fortunate to win many awards for this.

I've also done, and still do, lots of counselling for private clients and worked for several years for *Surestart* the government funded body for parents with young children working two days a week caring for the parents who's lives were in a sad state.

Looking back it was such a fun time and there were so many memorable occasions. There was a time when I was singing at a concert in Johnny and Cleo Lanes' place. George Melly was also on the bill. He came up and said how much he'd always wanted to meet me, especially after I had done a certain piece of art work. It involved filling a tray with blue/black ink and then drawing a piece of paper over it. On standing up to get the paper he said he could see the butterfly on the front of my knickers under my short skirt! The trouble is, he was right, there was a butterfly on my pants! I never did anything like that again, and stuck to wearing trousers!!

My philosophy working in childrens TV was always be truthful and always think that there is one child at the end of the camera who is in a room on his own and hasn't had anyone to talk to for a while. That way you really go through the lens and talk directly to everyone. I use this technique regardless of it being a kids programmes or an adult one."

For more information about Toni or for any projects please visit www.toniarthur-hay.com

The Glipton Giants never knew what had hit them when Jossy Blair came to town! This comedy football drama penned by legendary sports commentator Sid Waddell saw the trials and tribulations of a boys football team in the North East who became known as Sissy's Antjog, sorry I mean *Jossy's Giants*.

"My agent had sent me a script breakdown and they needed someone with a Geordie accent. I was frequently packed off to my grandmother's in South Shields when I was a lad so I was 'bi-lingual' in Geordie from a very early age.

I turned up for the audition and it was such a rainy day. I used to ride a motorbike then, and I'd staggered in dripping wet, with my helmet on and wax jacket looking very sorry and I read for the part of Jossy. I got to know Sid and he told me later I'd got the part as soon as I'd walked through the door as I looked such a mess, and Sid saw Jossy as a similarly ill-organised, dishevelled character.

Sid was a great bloke to have around once the filming started as he wasn't precious about his material, and sometimes actors have an instinct for 'what works' as dialogue. John Judd (Bob), Chris Burgess (Albert), Jennie McCracken (Glenda) and myself (the four regular characters) would take the same train every Monday from Euston to Manchester (where the series was produced). The four of us would read the script for that week and make changes which we felt were more appropriate to our characters. Sid said it didn't matter what we did with it, so long as his name was on the credits at the end! The fact is, *Jossy's Giants* was very much Sid's series. He came up with some very funny plots and characters drawn from his experiences as a Soccer 'dad'. He also wrote a series based on his son's cricket team called *Sloggers*.

Before Jossy, I worked mainly as an actor is small-scale touring companies. In the 70's and 80's you couldn't turn round without bumping into another Transit van full of actors, costumes and scenery. It was all great fun and I think we did some pretty good shows for people who didn't normally go to the theatre. I also did some stand up comedy at the Comedy Store where I met Rik Mayall and that group of comics. Rik was a very funny guy, and his act was of this pseudo-intellectual poet with a Churchillian V sign, and when he and the others went on to do *The Young Ones* any of the other comedians on at the Comedy Store turned up in the show too.

I went on to do various other TV, radio, film and theatre roles, including two years at the National Theatre in Alan Ayckbourn's *A Small Family Business*. It was a good two years which provided a steady income while my children were growing up.

My favourite role was Jossy, but I also appeared in G.F.Newman's TV play *The Nation's Health* which was about the NHS. I thought this was a seminal piece of television, like *Law and Order* (also by G.F. Newman).The plot was highly critical of some of the NHS practices. (and 'practises', for that matter). It was only shown once then disappeared without trace. Perhaps it's due for another screening.

I enjoy acting and prefer roles which have are a bit of a challenge and have some substance to them, and one such role was when I played the Earl of Gloucester in King Lear for the American Drama Group, which toured extensively around Europe and South America, performing in countries such as Germany and Costa Rica. It was quite a challenge but interesting to do.

I'm still working as a freelance actor, and in recent years I've appeared in *My Family, New Tricks, 50 Degrees North, Blessed* and *After You've Gone* for the BBC.

As a lad I didn't see a television until I was six years old. My Mum and Dad were members of the Communist Party and in the early 50s they were invited to the Czech Embassy and children were allowed to come along, and that TV in the Embassy was my first experience of watching television: the programme was *Muffin the Mule!"*

JIM BARCLAY

BEN BAZELL
PLAY SCHOOL

Among the plethora of *Play School* presenters Ben was very recognisable. Not only for his deep resonating tones but for his watch with the thick leather strap. Yes! Him! Ben twice made *Play School* history, and what is more, as a child, I was also fascinated by the Z in his surname...

"Bazell is actually an English name although it sounds quite exotic. We looked into our ancestry and there was a Richard Bazell who lived in Hampstead in the late 1600s. He was a farmer and he'd been given permission by the King to mint his own coins with his name on them, which he could give to the labourers on the farm. His wife was Dorothy, and my father and his sister were also called Dorothy and Richard. My dad started his working life as a chimney sweep – the family has gone downhill since!

Before I started *Play School* I was actually playing Rocky in the *Rocky Horror Show* at the Kings Road Theatre! So it was rather an odd change of circumstances, but the different jobs you get is one of the beauties of being an actor.

Play School was a lot of fun to do. The producer at the time was Anne Goby and I presented the show for 5 years in total. It was always a quick turnaround, filming 5 shows in a week and recorded as live. As it happens I went to a school in Tufnell Park with another well known *Play School* presenter, Derek Griffiths and we've been friends ever since then.

Theatre has always been my background and filming *Play School* allowed time to do other work, as you were only hired for every batch of programmes, there weren't any long contracts so I was free to do more theatre work, something which eventually took over my time. Besides, I couldn't go on being a kids TV presenter forever! I was 31 or 32 when I started *Play School* and I was one of the younger ones! Back then we were adults talking to a child, but presenters are a lot younger now and it seems they are being more childlike. It was often thought that we used to use phrases such as 'Let's do this' and 'We can do this' but this was never the case, it was always 'You' and 'Me' and not 'We', as the overriding piece of advice was to speak as if you were talking to a single child and not a mass audience.

I have a couple of *Play School* claims to fame. I presented the first same sex edition along with Ben Thomas. Up until then, it had always been one male and one female presenter, and it was a big thing at the time. I was also in the programme where the *Play School* clock stopped for the last time. At the end of recording an episode, an electrician walked onto the set and announced that this couldn't go on. We finished the take, the clock was on it podium, and it was switched off. There had been an ongoing dispute between two unions, and the Electricians Union, who wouldn't let it be operated if it wasn't by a Union man, pulled the plug on it. They tried ways to get round this dispute, not having a clock at all at one point, but in the end it was just ditched. It was a full blown heavy dispute over who flicked a switch!

I used to get recognised in the street quite often by young mums, firemen, taxi drivers...and I'd also be recognised by my watch with the big leather strap. I've still got the watch. It was actually my father's watch and as I ride a bike a lot it would get jolted around a lot and now it's in a delicate condition, but it still works.

My wife was pregnant, expecting our daughter while I was working on *Play School*, and the week before I was due to start recording I came off my bike and landed on my head. I had a huge swelling on my front temple which really hurt – I looked a bit like the elephant man. I thought to myself 'Oh my God, I won't be able to do *Play School*' and I called them up to explain what had happened, and they said it was a bit late in the day to get someone else and asked me to come in so they could take a look. They decided if they shot me from the front and not the side they could get away with it, and so there I was with a bandage on my head and dark glasses (as I'd got two huge black eyes as well). I looked like I'd been a few rounds with Henry Cooper! I think the news of my accident sent my wife into labour. Ironically, that was the week I had to ride a penny farthing around the studio.

I had a call at the studio and a message was passed to me 'Your wife has had a baby girl. Can you stand camera right?'

My daughter Katie was born – a child of *Play School*! She had some bruising around her eyes and the Sister said 'She has her father's eyes.' I then had to explain that my eyes were not usually like that!

I've had quite a few jobs in my career that I've enjoyed doing and amongst my theatre work I did a 3 year tour with the English Shakespeare Company which helped me see the world and hugely enjoyed being with the Pip Simmons Theatre Group and Bubble Theatre.

I am very proud of my three children, Tim who is a musician, Matthew who does a variety of jobs has just written a book about the state of English football and Katie who works in the theatre on the technical side.

I am heavily involved in Off The Page! Theatre Company these days and I do a one man show about the English poet John Clare."

You can catch up with Ben's current work and watch clips of his one man show at www.offtp.org.uk

BEN BAZELL

COLIN BENNETT

MR. BENNETT – TAKE HART, HART BEAT

I never saw eye to eye with my dad, and the fact that he found Mr. Bennett completely annoying pleased me no end! Of course, he was supposed to be and the purist in me should have been horrified at his attempts to disrupt the master at work, but I enjoyed the slapstick and seeing Mr. Bennett getting his comeuppence in the end.

"I am no legend of kids TV! In fact, really, the kid's TV with which I was associated didn't even make it into the top 100 children's programmes! Tony barely made it into bottom ten I think. A disgrace! He should have been knighted! But that's life. We had some great days.

I was an actor. I did very well for the first 20 years of my career. One of the great shows I did was *The Songwriters* a look at the musical legends of the previous Century (at that time the previous century was the Victorian's turn), I think it must have been about 1977. We used to shoot it at BBC Television Centre. One lunch time an old man tried to steal my HP sauce. During the ensuing fight I discovered that he was Christopher Pilkington the Producer/Director/Editor of *Hart Beat*, *Vision On* and *Take Hart*, though not in that order or all at the same time. He liked the suit I was wearing and wondered if they could borrow it for the show. I said, 'Where that suit goes, I go.' So... Mr Bennett and the suit were both hired on the very vague thought that I was allowed to go to Mr Hart's Studio and fall over on a regular basis. I still own the suit, though I hardly ever wear it now, except for best.

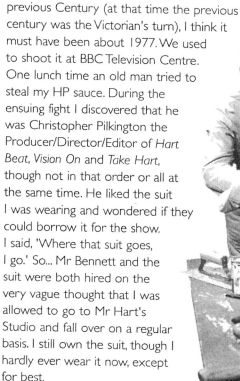

TONY HART & MR. BENNETT

Tony Hart, I have to say he was the nicest man I've ever met. I have to say that, but, of course, the truth is never out there. He spent 10 years dropping paint on my head, refusing to put my art in the Gallery and making me unblock drains! (for this I studied at RADA?!)

However, we often had to stop recording because we were laughing so much. Doesn't seem funny now but those were the olden days, we had simpler tastes. Sometimes, we were laughing so much they had to give in, not bother to try and get it right, and leave them in the show. Many times, in various episodes, you can see Tony and I trying to keep... not very straight faces.

I've had a great acting career, doing stuff like *Last of the Summer Wine*, *Hitch Hiker's Guide to the Galaxy*, *Ripping Yarns*, and years of theatre of which I guess the high spot was starring in the original West End production of *Chicago*,

playing Billy Flynn. Other notable screen faces I pulled were for the *There may be Trouble Ahead* singing commercial on finding my wife's pregnancy testing kit, for Allied Dunbar. I also had a birthday, in my attic, with my train set, saying the immortal line, 'Oh, Hello, Ben' when he gave me a signal box, found through Yellow pages. More recently I loved doing *Night Shift* with Graham Daniels of which we made 150 episodes. I have mainly been a TV Producer for the last 20 years making docos' like *Strictly Soho* and the Iconic, though never noticed, 28 half hour episodes of *Shoot the Writers!* a comedy sketch show peaking often at 2.1 million viewers post midnight for ITV1.

I am just about to publish my latest book *Acting on Television* which should be out by Christmas (I've already sold one copy... to a friend admittedly but it's a start) I also teach TV stuff at R.A.D.A. during the Summers.

My favourite TV Programme from the time was the great talent quiz show *You Should be So Lucky* hosted by the loathsome Vince Purity. It was an 'end of the pier' kind of act which made children compete on a giant snakes and ladders board to win the chance to perform their audition piece. An early incarnation of 'Britain's got Academy X.' Though I haven't yet ever met anyone else who saw it. The viewing figures were very good. So I imagine anyone who saw it, decided it was better to pretend they hadn't.

I am currently working in the Theatre and have four plays, as a writer, in pre-production. A new production of my 1986 play: *Hancock's Finest Hour*, plus *A life of Lenin*, and a couple of very strange plays, one called *The Accident Man* about a serial killer and *Dancing into the Light* a dance/musical exploration of the mysteries of life itself! And to bring you right up to date I'm in *Katie Brand's Big Ass Show*.

My tip to getting on telly...If you are an actor... go to drama School. You'll love it.

You can catch up with Colin's current work at www.acquiredtastetv.co.uk

Postscript: Tony Hart

Tony Hart's gone! It's the end of an era, it certainly is for me, and I guess for lots of people who seemed to share growing up with him. I was lucky enough to call him my friend for at least 30 years, and that began years after I had spent my childhood watching and marvelling at Vision On. I was lucky enough to work with him for many years and then share some of the last years after he had finished his TV career. I wish we had drunk much more tea together. It's hard to find the words that express how great a loss he is. **I think he was more influential than Van Gogh**. In fact, you can name any great influential artist and to four or five generations of British school children (not to mention the repeats around the World) he was the one who showed us that art was for everyone. **He should have been knighted,** but I guess the established art world didn't approve of simple, clean, childlike innocent art. And that's why his passing is so much the end of an era. He was a real gentleman, polite, good natured, always friendly, always interested, always encouraging and a great artist. With current Television seemingly obsessed by feeding us with Freak Show TV there is no place for a gentle talented ordinary good person. The World, more and more, loses its way as we lose that generation of people who knew what was right, and wasn't afraid to stand up to what was wrong. Sorry not to share funny anecdotes with you, I just can't do it at the moment. We must do our best to live better lives just like he would have wanted. As a special favour to me and in memory of Tony Hart please treat everyone you meet better than you would expect to be treated yourself... and please be polite. It's what he believed, and really the world will be a better place in which to live. It's that simple. Best wishes Colin (Mr.) Bennett.

DAVE BENSON PHILLIPS
PLAYDAYS, GET YOUR OWN BACK

Dave Benson Phillips has entertained a whole generation of children and is a hero to many after more than a decade of gunging adults, teachers and parents alike - plus the occasional celebrity!

During his career he's also been instrumental in creating awareness of Makaton, a basic sign language for people with communication and learning difficulties, and what's more, in August 2005, Dave was inducted into the Children's Walk of Fame. Respect to the gunge pool!!

"I'd been working on the holiday camps for quite a while and one of them was Haven Leisure. They sent me to a holiday camp called Ty Mawr in North Wales where I was working as a children's entertainer. In those days they used to be called a 'Children's Uncle'. By and large I'd been spotted by some people who were on holiday who had some contact with the BBC and said 'You should come along and see this guy, he entertains the children etc ...' I got a letter from the BBC asking if I could come in for an audition and I went to the BBC and entertained the secretaries and staff at the office for a couple of hours. They said 'Thank you very much for coming', but didn't hear much from then until a couple of months later, when I got a letter from the BBC, saying 'Would you like to go into a programme called Play School?'

I said 'Yesssssss!' and we all had a massive party at Mirrors, a nightclub just down the road from the holiday camp. However, everything went very quiet. Play School had actually been taken off the air... I was gutted. But there was another show being developed called Playdays (or Play Bus as it was known originally), and I went along for an audition for that and they invited me to appear on that show instead. That was my first foray into TV. Usually people get a years contract but because I was so inexperienced I was given a contract for six weeks! I ended up appearing on Playdays for six years, so that was kinda cool.

I've been fortunate to have a long career in children's television, and long may it continue until I'm old enough to retire! It's been such an incredible thing to be associated with such great programmes. Some people are lucky if they get one or two programmes, and I've had quite a few which people have wanted to watch, and I'm very thankful of that. I never thought I was a watchable person at all, I'm not handsome, I'm not sexy, I'm not gorgeous, so I'm thankful if people do say they watch me, or make an appointment to watch me.

Get Your Own Back ran for about 14 years, and I think the reason why it was so successful was that the format was the same no matter what happened. We had a child on there who wanted to reek revenge on the grown up who they thought had wronged them and basically they wanted to humiliate the grown up and get them covered in gunge at the end, which is what they all worked towards. The adults were always the victims. Over the years the gunge just got bigger. At the beginning we had a chair that would drop the grown-up into the tank, and towards the end we had a complete slide which threw people into a fair few tons of gunge at the bottom. Children love seeing that! There's something about the whole slide which appeals to children. Even now I still get messages from children about getting their own back on some grown up!!

Noel Edmonds and Crinkley Bottom were marvellous at gunging. They had things like a dodgem car and we wanted something like this for Get Your Own Back. Unfortunately children's television has to work with very small budgets. Whereas Noel had a dodgem car with gunge tanks above their heads, we had to justify to the powers that be why we needed to have a slide. After all, things like that tend to be very expensive, not to mention the issues of safety. Some of the BBC personnel asked 'Couldn't we just have them walk into it or slip into it?' to which we'd reply "No, no, noooo" because we wanted a bit of drama, but we were spurred on because the nation's children loved the show. The money was spent, the slide was made and Get Your Own Back was up and running.

When we did the first series we got about a thousand letters sent to us wanting people to be gunged, and

DAVE BY THE GUNGE POOL

another series, we put out an advert with our address, thinking nothing of it, and we had about 250,000 people a year replied saying 'Can you do this?', 'Can you come round to my house? You don't even have to do anything stupid, just come round to my house!' It got very huge. Very very huge.

Get Your Own Back finished because it was a question of economics. No one has actually turned to me and said it's completely dead, they've always said 'watch this space' so I remain hopeful that there will be another series. Watch this space...

I received loads of advice, some of its constructive, for instance to remember to look down the middle of the camera lens when talking to the viewer. If you imagine a camera lens to be like the rings of a tree You HAVE to look right in the centre ring. I was so inexperienced, so green. If you looked at the outer edge of the centre ring, it looks like you're not looking at them, and that piece of advice was like a lightbulb moment for me. I had loads of moments like that. 'Read the script' was another one! A lot of presenters, until they become comfortable in front of the lens, have a nervous trait. Mine was doing a Stevie Wonder-type movement, moving side to side. The cameramen said it used to make them feel ill!! Talking to children is a great, positive thing, but there was one person who said 'Oh, don't do it!'

I'd always wanted to be on TV, but had no training in it. I had no clue. I used to watch a LOT of children's programmes when I was a child, my mum used to say to me 'Your eyes will go square'. She also said to me 'You'll never be on it if you keep watching it' which was kinda wise. I used to watch *Play School* when I was very young, but the one that really did it for me is *Sesame Street*. I'd love to make a British version of it. I have a lot of favourites, but for me, that was the benchmark TV programme. It was for children of any age. It was multi-levelled, multi-faceted, taught the alphabet and numbers, had interaction with humans, had animation and puppetry, there was reinforcement through songs, appearances by celebrities, always enforcing the ideals of learning and that you're on a planet with loads of different people with loads of different backgrounds. It was just fab! I also grew up with *Star Trek* (the original series), loved the sci-fi and nature programmes too.

I've managed to work with my heroes. I worked as an usher at The Polka Theatre, Wimbledon. I saw Toni Arthur's folk shows and I was an usher when Rod, Jane and Freddy performed there. I had a serious crush on Jane. She looked fine on the TV, but in real life she was amazing. She's just gorgeous! I also entertained the troops with Fred Harris. We we working for a military TV channel SSVC and we were a musical duo, Fred on the bass and me on the guitar, and we were in a field in the middle of Germany giving it our all to the NATO forces and families. We were the support act for Bronski Beat who were in the tent next door! Very rock and roll!! I also did a children's party for Brian Cant's children. Now that was fab!! We even performed a show together. It makes me smile when I think about it. I've also worked with Richard Vobes at Chessington World of Adventures. It's great that I've worked with people that I used to watch, and kinda humbling.

We live in a time when, if the TV executives get the money wrong or they don't get enough viewing figures, the programmes can disappear. I spent a time living in Barbados and their children's output was just from 5.30 - 6.00pm every day!

Children still write to me. A lot of them have their own children now, and that's the freaky thing, but I like it."

To hire Dave Benson Phillips for television/film/video appearances and production, radio, music and voice works, corporate stuff, theatre shows & pantomime, The W.I.T. fund-raising initiative, event-hosting & personal appearances, bouncy castles/inflatables, creche facilities and play areas for hire, musical concerts, MAKATON, gunge gameshows, after-dinner speaking and a host of other events please visit www.davebensonphillips.co.uk or call +44(0)1903-248-258. Give yourself a hug for reading this bit!

DAVE BENSON PHILLIPS

BOB BLOCK
CREATOR & WRITER - RENTAGHOST

If your mansion house needs haunting...who better to create and write one of the most popular tales of ghosts and ghouls and freaks and fools than Mr. Bob Block — one of the unheralded legends of kids TV. A prolific writer for the likes of Ken Dodd and Dave Allen, Bob created a legendary series that is still popular and fondly remembered to this day.

BOB IN THE ARMY

"I served with the Royal Army Service Corps during the war and afterwards, I worked as a mechanic for the Fire Brigade in Wickham, Hampshire. I always felt I had a talent for writing and so, encouraged by my wife Madeline I wrote some comedy sketches and sent them to Ted Kavanar, Derek Roy's agent. Derek Roy was one of biggest radio stars of the day in the 1940s and 50s and at the time I sent the scripts to him, he had a popular radio show *Hip Hip Hoo Roy*. He also used to regularly host Variety Bandbox and I felt Roy's humour fitted very well with my style of writing.

Roy and his agent wrote back to me saying they felt I had great talent, but to consider carefully if I wanted to follow the writer's path, saying "Remember that you may have to churn out the same work week after week..." They were careful to point out, though, that this was not to discourage me, just to be realistic.

I went down to Portsmouth to see Roy performing and to meet him, and much to his delight Roy said he wanted to use some of my sketches on *Variety Bandbox*!

So this was how I started — in radio. I was invited to write for the Lyons family in *Life With The Lyons* which started on radio, but went onto TV in the 60s, and that then got me into television circles.

As well as those shows, I also cut my teeth writing for *Radio Rinso, Starlight Hour, Festival of Britain* and *Arthur's Inn* on the radio in the 50s and then *Our House* and *Discord In Three Flats* in the 60s before moving onto television writing. After writing for *That's My Boy, Crackerjack, Hey Presto It's Rolf, Frost*

Over England, The Mavis Branston Show (in Australia), Kindly Leave The Stage, Broaden Your Mind, Ken Dodd And The Diddymen, The Dave King Show and The Dave Allen Show, I wanted to start making use of my own ideas. Like all writers, I had a vivid imagination and many, many ideas for shows. I was always a huge fan of sci-fi (Arthur C. Clarke was my particular favourite author). I was, by the early 70s, respected enough in the industry to be able to put forward my own storylines and the first one to be made was Pardon My Genie in 1972 and '73. Robert's Robots was then produced in 1973 and '74, leading the way for the most successful of all — Rentaghost. All of the characters in Rentaghost were designed to complement each other and slot into the storylines to create interesting scripts and so the different magic powers of each ghost were created to bring the most comedy to the episodes. Those characters who didn't have names that described their powers were mostly taken from friends and family!

I never really received any advice for writing for children, but would always say to those contemplating the task 'DO NOT write down to them or patronise them!' It's something that an awful lot of people in Children's TV do and it is nearly always their downfall!

I'm probably most proud of Rentaghost because it was conceived and written by myself alone for the full nine series and nine years of its run and it's become one of the most favourite children's shows of the all time, let alone the 1970s! I always got a lot of correspondence from children and would-be writers all over the world due to Rentaghost and that made me very proud.

There are many stories about my years in 'the business', but one short one that involved the actress and great friend to myself and my wife (and Godmother to my daughter Trish) Molly Weir, who I initially worked with when she played the housekeeper Aggie in Life With The Lyons

BOB AT WORK

and whom I then wrote the part of Hazel the McWitch for in *Rentaghost*. She was very proud of being a 'canny' scot and being 'carefull with the baubies' and in fact was renowned for it! In the late 70s she had written another book of her recipes and one day she turned up to rehearsals for *Rentaghost* with a pile of her brand new books. 'There's one for everyone' she said. All the actors were delighted and went over to her to collect their copy. When the first person put their hand out with profuse thanks, Molly said 'That'll be £3.95 dear please...'! This was of course the full retail price! She was, however, in reality the biggest hearted person you could find and actually very generous to those less fortunate. She left over a million pounds in her will to various charities.

As for my own childhood, I was born in 1921 when there was no television so my favourite children's programmes were obviously from the radio! Even then there was very little choice and my own memories are of Children's Hour, which started broadcasting in 1922."

BOB BLOCK

RICHARD BRIERS OBE CBE
ROOBARB & CUSTARD, NODDY

A green dog and a purple cat, it can only be *Roobarb & Custard*. Created by cartoonist Grange Calveley and brought to life by the quirky animation of Bob Godfrey and the narration of Richard Briers. Richard has also lent his vocal skills to narrating *Noddy*, being Bob the Builder's dad, and starring as the rabbit 'Fiver' in the classic heart-wrenching animated film *Watership Down*. What a good life!

"I think I've always had a feel for children's stuff, an empathy for kids stories, maybe because I've never really grown up! I'd been the voice of *Noddy* and a character in *Wind in the Willows* on audio tape, and was known as a kids entertainer on the side.

The creator of *Roobarb and Custard*, Grange Calveley was a brilliant guy, he wanted someone to do the voices and I'd always thought of myself as a fairly good reader, and I met with him after reading the scripts and he started doing these voices. This was some 30 years ago when *Roobarb & Custard* was first broadcast.

When the new series came about, Grange was living in Australia and he enquired if I was still alive to do some more episodes. It was tiring work having to do so many different characters and female voices. They also wanted a welsh mole voice but I'm not so good with dialects so I was wondering what I could do. In the end I thought of doing an impression of Richard Burton!

In total I recorded 30 episodes of *Roobarb & Custard* with a 30 year gap in between!

I went on to appear in *The Good Life* and *Ever Decreasing Circles*, and back in those days there was more rehearsal time to learn lines at home.

I like the black and white era of *Doctor Who*. My wife, the actress Ann Davies, played a character called Jenny in a William Hartnell episode *The Dalek Invasion of Earth* in 1964.

I played the Chief Caretaker in *Paradise Towers* opposite Sylvester McCoy's Doctor in 1987. The director kept telling me not to overact, but at that time, that's how evil characters were seen to be like, so how could I not overact?

I also had a part in the Dr Who spin-off *Torchwood* playing opposite Burn Gorman who is a brilliant actor. It was a great experience but there was more rehearsal time in the old days, now you just have to turn up and do it.

As for the new *Doctor Who*, I thought David Tennant was too young, at first, as I prefer the Doctor as an older character, but he's grown on me. He's terrific!

I enjoy watching *Midsomer Murders* and *The Simpsons*. I'm a great fan of the animator Nick Park and my favourite programme on TV is *Shaun the Sheep*!"

RICHARD BRIERS

SIMON BUCKLEY
NOBBY THE SHEEP, BEAR BEHAVING BADLY

One of the many unsung legends of kids TV, Simon Buckley, has had a hand in the success of many kids TV shows – quite literally! The skillful art of puppeteering is something that doesn't necessarily get the recognition that it deserves, but without these skilled performers, the characters we love would not be brought to life.

"I became a puppeteer as a result of my grand parents buying me Sooty and Sweep glove puppets at the age of four! Sweep was my particular favourite and many family photographs were ruined or enhanced by his appearance in the picture. At the age of eight I saw some Pelham puppets hanging in the window of the Arts and Crafts Studio, a rather grandly named toy shop in Chester, and I immediately fell in love with them and was overjoyed to receive the Wizard for Christmas. Saving up my pocket money I quickly bought other Pelham Puppet characters and aged nine was asked to perform at a class mate's birthday party for which I was paid one pound. The following day a stranger phoned up and asked my father if she could speak to Simon Buckley the children's party entertainer 'well, you can' he said 'but he's only nine', 'that's okay', she replied, 'he's only a pound!' The bookings started rolling in, and in the year I turned 16 I performed just over a hundred shows at birthday parties, fetes and fairs.

My first love was always marionettes, having grown up with Bill and Ben and the wooden tops (though I wasn't keen on Andy Pandy who I thought was a bit wet!). But the arrival of the muppets on television broadened

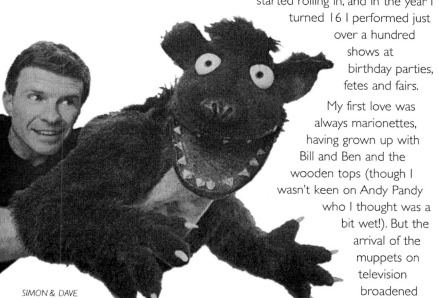

SIMON & DAVE
THE HYENA

LITTLE JOE

my interests to other kinds of puppets beyond the traditional, though the thought of working in television and performing to a camera rather than an audience didn't initially appeal. Of course I've massively revised that opinion and love to work for television.... And also have discovered that particularly when doing risqué out-takes cameramen and the crew on the studio floor make the best audience there is! As the musical *Avenue Q* proves each night, everyone loves to see puppets being rude, and making children's television gives rather a lot of opportunity for that in between takes.

Puppets in television have gone, and continue to grow through metamorphoses in terms of styles and fashions – one minute puppets are out and CGI is in, then everyone wants Tellytubby type suits, then the pendulum swings back again. Often in the quest to make a puppet innovative and unique a new material will be used or the puppet head will be crammed full of animatronic features, which 9/10 are totally unnecessary. I always look to Kermit the frog – a bit of Jim Hensons' mother's coat and two ping pong balls and recognise just about the most expressive puppet of all times. How inspired to film him doing a tap dance to happy feet and not even need to see his legs! Most puppeteers and producers would now want to build special rigs to move separate legs etc, but for me the genius of a good puppet character (and puppeteer!) is the bringing to life of something very simple. I much prefer small simple puppets that make people ask 'so, it's really just your hand in there???'

The fact that the puppeteer, as a personality, is largely never recognised or becomes a household name is an interesting one, and for me, most of the time a positive rather than a negative aspect of the business – I don't get asked for autographs when out having dinner with friends or stared at in the street. When I was performing Nobby The Sheep on *Ghost Train* (a character from Saturday morning kids TV I did for 6 years) I did start to resent all the adulation the presenters got, and whilst Nobby got more fan mail than the rest of the team put together I was very much Nobby's No-body! Arriving in a limo for Jason Donovan's 21st birthday party in Kensington the *Ghost Train* presenters and I were greeted by a hoard of photographers who kindly asked me to step out of the way! I'm sure if I had taken the sheep along with me I'd have been in the centre of the picture rather than holding my colleagues coats at the side. However 18 years on I am still in demand for TV shows and they, who had their moment of fame, are who knows where?

I am concerned at the way children's television is being undermined in this share-driven, commercially biased world. We are making less original products, but some good programmes continue to come through - *In The Night Garden* being a shining example, not least for its clearly defined characters which are apparently simple but have such great personalities. Maca Paca rocks! In terms of puppetry in children's television *Book of Pooh* is superb and, with *Bear in the Big Blue House*, work I really admire. I'd love there to be another *Fraggle Rock*, or *Spooks of Bottle Bay* – it's been ages since we had a TV show with a proper cast of puppets inhabiting their own environment, rather than them being guests in the human world – though when used well (and I am proud to add BBC/Darrall Macqueen's *Bear Behaving Badly* to that category) it is a vindication of the power of the puppet to see them hold their own. As someone said recently during a take 'How the hell am I being upstaged by the equivalent of a f**cking sock and a couple of buttons??!!!'.

You can read more about Simon's work on his website www.simonbuckley.co.uk

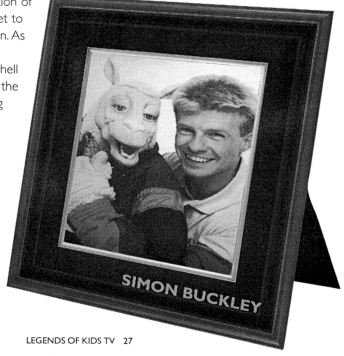

SIMON BUCKLEY

BOB CAROLGEES
TISWAS

Amongst the anarchy and chaos of TISWAS, Bob Carolgees started as a guest and eventually ended up as a full blown presenter. With his monkey puppet Charlie, and his comic 'psychic' Houdi Elbow, Bob became a popular face on Saturday morning TV, but let's not forget his most famous creation – the puppet dog that spat its way into the nation's hearts.

"I had been working my cabaret act (which developed from me fronting a mobile disco around merseyside for many years) around the working mens clubs for several years when I was spotted working at the Fords Club in Liverpool by Ken Dodd, the outcome of that is that I worked solidly with 'Doddy' for eighteen months, so now I was being seen by much more important bookers etc.

This was followed by being bottom of the bill at my first major summer season, in Torquay for Cilla Black. For the following few years I was working my way up the bill on various seasonal shows with some of the big names of the day, I had done some work with Frank Carson, it was he who took me to *TISWAS* and introduced me to Chris Tarrant, within two weeks I was invited to join the team.

We went on to do *OTT*, then *Saturday Stayback*. I then fronted a series from Alton Towers for three years called *Hold Tight*.

I was then invited to co-host *Surprise Surprise* with Cilla which I gladfully did for eight years. During all this time I also hosted the game show, *Concentration*, did many, many one off variety shows and specials, and was one of the foremost entertainers for our troops around the world, as well as fronting major adverts for Hellmans Mayonnaise (8 years) and various others."

Bob now owns and runs a candle shop which you can visit at www.carolgeescandles.com

MICHAEL & JOANNE COLE
FINGERBOBS, BOD, RAGTIME, HEADS & TAILS...

If ever there was anyone who did more than most to influence a generation, it must be Michael & Joanne Cole. Sadly departed, these two creative genius's brought us a number of well loved shows, and should be heralded as such. Michael and Joanne's work is remembered through the eyes of their son Lo.

"My parents were always busy creating. My father was either writing or searching for a fresh idea, and my mother was always sketching or sewing something. And it was this combination of creative talent and enthusiasm that was to enthral a whole generation of pre-school children and to transform our childhood: mine along with my two sisters, Alison and Kate, and my brother Sam. We were raised in Sussex but were later to move to London as our parents got more and more involved in the various projects that punctuated our lives. Among some of their most favourite creations, characters such as *Bod* and *Fingermouse* have endured and are now firmly established as icons of the so-called 'golden age' of children's TV.

In the early 60's our parents started to create children's books together. They developed a number of unpublished 'dummy' books — one of which was Bod. At that time they were seeking to create something more meaningful and in tune with the way children think — with a different type of philosophy to the Blyton-like tales that were currently in vogue. Inspired by Taoist literature and Chinese art, Picasso's fauns and Surrealism, *Bod* was developed and eventually published by Methuen books in 1965. Originally there were just the four titles, 'Bod's Apple', 'Bod's Present', 'Bod and the Cherry Tree', and 'Bod's Dream.' Bod lived in a minimal space along with his four friends, Aunt Flo, PC Copper, Frank the Postman and Farmer Barleymow. Together they had quiet

MICHAEL COLE

adventures; waiting for an apple to fall from the sky or discovering a giant bowl of strawberries and cream at the bottom of a hole in the ground.

My father's previous experience in advertising, his simple, witty scripts and stories, and the originality and depth of his ideas and their ability to connect gained him full time employment at the BBC, writing scripts for *Play School*.

JOANNE COLE

From here he went on to direct and produce his own programmes for the BBC TV series, *Watch With Mother* as well being on the team of writers for *Play School's* older sister, *Playaway*.

In 1971 my parents were working on a show called *Fingerbobs*. The 15 minute episodes revolved around a guru-like bearded Canadian (Rick Jones) who played the part of Yoffy. In each episode Yoffy would enlist the assistance of his friend, Fingermouse (who was a rolled up cone of paper wrapped around a finger with two floppy ears). The show was literally hands-on, finger puppets made from paper all ingeniously created by my mother, whose purpose was to collect material in order for Yoffy to tell his story. I remember being surrounded by what seemed like hundreds of Fingermice with re-enforced noses, as my parents worked night and day to meet their deadlines. A proud moment was when my foot was enlisted to kick a football on the film set, with Fingermouse scampering furiously around it.

Among other shows from this period produced for *Watch With Mother*, my parents made *Ragtime* in 1973 (the characters all being wooden spoons and made from rags), which received a BAFTA award and, of course, *Bod*, who made his TV debut in 1975. When my father received his award from Princess Anne, the ceremony was live on ITV. He claimed his trophy during the adverts (on account of pre-school audiences not being that important) so I never did see it, but he does look very proud in the photograph.

More books and programmes followed. If my mother wasn't doing comic strips of *Fingerbobs* for Pippin magazine, she was working on new book ideas that my father had written. *Gran* was one of those, based loosely on my great-grand mother, who my mother adored. The idea became a set of books and a TV series animated by Ivor Wood.

Other projects include *Choc-A-Bloc* (which must have passed me by as I have hardly any recollection of this) and *Heads and Tails*. I loved *Heads and Tails* –

it was all about animals and shot entirely on location. Derek Griffiths provided the narration and brilliantly performed his own compositions of my father's lyrics which provided the soundtrack for the show. In one episode my daily routine walk of the dog on the green was filmed with me looking embarrassingly uncomfortable with 70's haircut and cowboy boots. My father also wrote *Pigeon Street*, which he made in collaboration with animator Alan Rogers who had previously worked on *Bod*.

By the early 80's my mother was ill with cancer. She was still working and this time it was because Fingermouse had been offered his own TV series. The mice had returned but now they were not confined to her studio as she had moved downstairs on account of her illness.

My father was to carry on working after her death in 1985 producing a number of unpublished novels and further reams of poetry (he was always writing poems).

In the early 90's he was asked by Carlton TV to develop a new TV series for pre-school audiences. He wrote, produced and directed *Alphabet Castle*, which was to capture the hearts of a new generation of young children. The agenda was to provide an educational context that was fun for under five's, and it delivered just that with many a song and silly rhyme performed by King Alpha and Queen Betty. The programme was so successful that it was immediately commissioned for a second series keeping my father very busy.

Before my fathers death in 2001 I remember how thrilled he was to see a gathering tide of young people fondly acknowledging the achievements of his and my mother's work. *Bod* was rated 36 in the top 100 all-time Childrens TV programmes on Channel 4 and *Fingerbobs* was No. 50. Fans had websites dedicated to the little bald character in the yellow dress who is now in endless demand on DVD. The under-fives have grown up, proving that pre-school memories and affections are life-transforming and pre-school audiences are important after all."

BOD

CHARLES COLLINGWOOD
WORDY - LOOK & READ

What's orange with no legs? No, not an orange. It's Mr. Watchword of course, Wordy for short. This high-pitched character with a passing resemblence to the ball element from an old fashioned typewriter, flew around the screen and helped me to look and read, and became a truly memorable creation. Look and Read's stories were also particularly memorable, none more so than *The Boy from Space*, with the curiously named alien Peep-Peep. From Haslemere to Ambridge, Charles has certainly been an all round entertainer.

"I've been involved with Schools TV for 20 years. Dorothea Brooking was a producer, alongside Claire Chovil, and she gave me my break. She wanted me to play an Italian gypsy in *Haslemere*. I asked her why me, and she said 'You can make me laugh for 3 weeks.' We got on famously and became best of friends.

On *Look and Read*, they wanted Wordy to be a bouncy character that flew around the studio, and I remembered Terry Scott used to do a little boy's voice, and so I slightly adapted that for Wordy's voice, it seemed appropriate for a character with no legs!

A lot of the filming was done in Bristol, and some in London. They created a little section in the studio for me, with the presenter on set, and I'd be behind a screen with a monitor and headphones and I worked to the pictures on my screen.

They needed someone small to fit in Wordy's costume and they mostly used an actress called Katie Hebb. She had her own set of headphones inside the costume so she could receive direction. The poor girl got very hot inside there. Early on, they had tried using a studio AFM, but on going to lunch, he used to go to the bar and have several pints, so when we resumed filming, the character was initially over animated, and later in the day he'd be nearly comatose!

The crew knew about my love of cricket, as they would always be filming the show during the cricket season. So, as my confidence grew, they gave me a monitor with the pictures from the cricket, so I could keep up to date with the scores whilst being professional and working.

I'd never set out to work specifically in children's TV. I was unemployed and I was given a chance, but to my great joy, one thing lead to another."

I met my wife, Judy Bennett, whilst I worked on *Words & Pictures*. Tony Robinson was the presenter and myself, along with Judy, Miriam Margolyes and Nigel Lambert were the voices for the puppets. We were four difficult people to control!

As an actor, I've diversified. My first ever role was as Estragon in *Waiting for Godot*. I also appeared in *Rosencrantz and Guildenstern Are Dead*, and I've enjoyed reading the news on the BBC World Service, co-hosted a game show with Bernard Manning, been the eccentric scorer on *Telly Addicts* with Noel Edmonds, done 20 *Call My Bluffs*, and *Just a Minute* as well as voices for other children's programmes such as *Cloppa Castle, The Munch Bunch* and *Here Comes Mumfie*. I'm probably best known for playing Brian Aldridge in the famous soap opera The Archers on Radio 4 since 1975.

The Head of Radio 4, Michael Green, spoke to me just after a picture of myself and the family had appeared in the Radio Times pictured by our pool and he said to me 'I didn't realise we were paying you enough to have a pool!' and I said "You don't, you pay for the chemicals. Wordy paid for the pool!"

When I was a child my parents were into comedy shows on the radio, such as Arthur Askey, but I didn't understand why people laughed at certain things. I began to realise that some people laughed because of nerves. I'd listen to their delivery and timing and I enjoyed that comics could sink or swim on their own ability. That's why I enjoy doing my one man show *Playing Away* it's the nearest I'll get to being a stand-up comedian.

I'm really lucky to have done what I've done but I'd quite like to host *Have I Got News for You*. I think I could be suitably pompous!"

Look out for Charles' autobiography "Brian & Me" published by Michael O'Mara Books, which is due out in October.

CHARLES COLLINGWOOD

PHIL CORNWELL
GET FRESH, GILBERT'S FRIDGE, KING STUPID

Phil Cornwell might be better known to some as a resident of Stella Street or an early morning DJ on Radio Norfolk, but Phil's ability for impersonations has seen him do a wealth of different work from a Rolling Stone to a big green snotty alien! Phil recalls what it was like to be Gilbert the alien, and how they are similar in some ways! Phil Cornwell – the man who sold the TARDIS!

"Prior to *Get Fresh* the *Vicious Brothers* (Angelo & Andy Smart) were on Saturday morning TV but the bosses wanted a change of route. It was Janet Street-Porter and the producer Michael Forte who had the idea to have an alien puppet and they commissioned the Spitting Image puppet makers Fluck & Law to make Gilbert. Incidentally, they use the lip mould from Ringo Starr's puppet for Gilbert's mouth! It was a big puppet and made a big impact on the small screen. A lot of the other TV puppets were small – Sooty, Basil Brush. Big characters, but small puppets.

I'd done some surreal stuff with my impressions on the cabaret circuit, Mike Yarwood was a hero of mine, but my act wasn't anything like his. Michael Fortes had seen one of my gigs and he got me in to have a try out.

The brief for Gilbert was that they wanted to give it a mad character and that his only influences of Earth was from TV and films and he had soaked up all that stuff, which is the same as what I did when I arrived from planet Phil! So it was perfect, and it was a good vehicle for me.

Gilbert was my first foray into kids TV, working alongside Charlotte Hindle and Gaz Top, who I'm still good friends with 20 years later. They had a script for their links, but mine was mostly improvised. I'd write little bits the night before and chuck them in whilst I chuntered away. I would freewheel it. It was live TV and was all part of the fun.

Kids would love the visual stuff – the KY Jelly coming out of Gilbert's nose (that's what we used!) but verbally it was aimed at a Saturday morning audience that were just sitting there, a bit hung over. I didn't really think about a kids audience, and I didn't patronise them, and I think that's why it worked.

There was a lot of adult stuff and I'm not sure that I could get away with some of the things I said these days. People of a certain age have fond memories of it!

I went onto work on *Spitting Image* – I only did one voice, that of Mick Jagger, but it's on my CV!

I like the variety of the work I do and embrace it and I enjoy doing good kids comedy shows (all of them seem to be at the BBC). I got to be *King Stupid* and when I go to the playground to pick up my kids, the other kids there will shout 'Look, its King Stupid!' and I say 'I do other stuff too!!' But whatever work I do, I always treat it the same no matter what.

Stella Street came about because Peter Richardson of Comic Strip fame had an idea to get me and John Sessions together to see what we could come up with. *The Comic Strip* were a disparate group, and I'd joined in the latter half of their run, in the 90s.

I'd previously worked with John Sessions in 1989 on a Radio 4 comedy show *Lenin of the Rovers* with Alexei Sayle and Jim Broadbent.

Keith Allen had mentioned me to Peter and I played the character Jimmy Twizzle in *The Crying Game* – a piss take on Paul Gascoigne – and Keith played Roy Brush. I went on to do another 4 Comic Strips before I did *The Glam Metal Detectives*.

I used to write sketches for it and appeared with Doon Mackichan, Gary Beadle, David Schneider, Sarah Stockdale and Paul Putner, but we only did one series. It was a very expensive show, and it was at a similar time to the *Fast Show*, which was great but a bit cheaper to make and so the BBC went with that.

So, myself and John came up with the whole of *Stella Street*. No one had done impersonations in that docu-soap sort of way before. I get great feedback from those who remember it.

It was great to be in 2 series of *Alan Partridge*. The one in the hotel and the static home, as Dave Clifton. It's one of those series that will always be there. 'Cone but not forgotten' you could say. Dave never had the last laugh. I added a little bit of improvised stuff but the producer Armando Iannucci is a shrewd bugger and was serious about the comedy because they wanted it to work, so it was quite strict.

I first met Steve Coogan in 1990 and we did a double act at the Amnesty International benefit in 1992 doing impressions – Steptoe and Son and the Mick Jagger brothers, and to top it off I got to introduce Spinal Tap!

I also did the narration with Barry Davies on the Stare Out competition on *Big Train*, and in other kids shows I've played an estate agent in *Danny's House*, a nun in *Hotel Trubble* with Arabella Weir, a bald guy taking over the world in *M.I. High* and soon to be an old spanish peasant woman with Dick & Dom.

It helps to have the gear on when being these characters. 'It starts with the shoes' is what the old actors used to say.

Doctor Who was a right buzz to do. I played a street merchant in the episode 'Fires of Pompeii' which fans have said is one of the great episodes. I was asked to do that role and its always nice to be asked. It was a lovely little jolly to Rome for a few days. It was beautifully done and it was on an amazing and enormous set which was just like ancient Rome. David Tennant was a nice fella.

One of the funniest guys I've ever met is John Thompson who's a great impressionist but he didn't really go down that route. John told me one of the funniest things I've ever heard. John Hurt was on location, and one morning, being hungover, he went down for breakfast in the hotel. He grumbled (with his best John Hurt voice) 'What have you got?', 'We can do you a boiled egg...' came the reply 'Oh, Christ!!!! I'll just have a boiled egg then!!'

I've had a great body of work. It's something to look back at when I have those days when I'm not working. I certainly would have taken it if it was offered to me in the early days."

BERNARD CRIBBINS
JACKANORY, THE WOMBLES, DR WHO

What is there to not love about Bernard Cribbins? A voice to a generation, whether it was wombling on Wimbledon Common or as a record breaking storyteller on *Jackanory*. And now, of course, he's made a huge impact yet again, this time as Donna Noble's dear old Grandad in Doctor Who. Bernard Cribbins — the Doctor's most faithful companion.

"My first *Jackanory* story was in black and white in the late 1960s. Molly Cox was the producer and I used one of those Pollacks Toy theatres for the story. The stage was cut out as well as the characters which were put on sticks. It was like a miniature Punch & Judy. I did all the voices and it was great fun.

I did 1 or 2 stories a year, and ended up doing a world record 111 episodes in total. The BBC didn't pay very much money but it didn't matter as there were some nice stories.

I got to tell the stories of *Alice in Wonderland* and *Wind in the Willows* and I also did a lot of Joan Aiken's stories with Mortimer the Raven. I was very fortunate to get a lot of nice stories, and I was able to be animated with each character and use my repertoire of 6 voices — then use them again for another story!

The BBC had a policy of reusing their tapes, and they wiped some of the early *Jackanory* stories, including a couple of mine, which is sad.

The show expanded and we did some stories on location. We went to the Mapledurham estate in Surrey for *Wind in the WIllows*, where the story was actually written, and I had to drive a 1910 Hotchkiss car, with its wooden steering wheel. I drove very gingerly along the towpath whilst telling the story as I didn't want to go into the canal! There I was in this silly blazer and a boater — you could dress for the part and move around and it got huge viewing figures.

Now, everything is about CGI and there doesn't seem to be enough faith in having someone sat one-to-one with the viewer and reading a story. I'm still certain if either myself, or Dame Judi Dench or the late Kenny Williams read a story, kids would sit and watch it. Kids are still the same as they used to be in the 70s, and one person looking into a lens is still good enough.

The Wombles was such a long time ago! I did a reading for my audition, and did 3 different silly voices at a time. Several different actors auditioned for it, and I was lucky enough to get it.

The making of The Wombles was a laborious process as it was stop-frame animation. It took 60 days to create 5 minute of the finished episode, but I came in after they'd done the animation and had a skeletal script with the storyline and I was allowed to fill in the gaps with noises - umms and ahhhs, or even 5 minutes of snoring for Orinocho!

I'd go into Filmfair, check the dialogue, write in some ad libs – it was a lovely job to do. The Wombles, along with Roobarb and Bagpuss still have a huge following and I can accurately age a person if they come up to me and say 'I used to watch the Wombles when I was 5 or 6.'

It was great to be asked to do David Tennant's last 2 Doctor Who specials and great fun to do – It's a ripper! We weren't given the end of the scripts so I don't even know what will happen at the end. I have to say, though, that the Cardiff team are the most wonderful unit to work with. The best TV film unit I've ever worked with in my whole career. They are absolutely brilliant. Better than any movie I've done. They've worked so hard and do it so well.

David is a brilliant leader of the pack, he's there, stands on his marks, says his lines and gets on with it. You haven't, at any time, got to wait for the 'star' to arrive. David will miss it enormously. 4 years is a long time, longer than usual for a Doctor, and a long time travelling up the M4!

The team of writers have produced some brilliant scripts. All the writers are good but Russell is a fantastic writer and I think they'll miss his writing.

David is a better Doctor than Peter Cushing's. Peter was a great guy to work with but his Doctor in the movie (Daleks' Invasion Earth: 2150 A.D.) was played as more bumbling and as if he was always chewing on an imaginary mint!

BERNARD CRIBBINS

We had our wrap part after the filming ended in May, and I was called up on stage and they gave me a picture as a momento. The top half was a picture of me with Peter Cushing from 1966 and the bottom half was a picture of me and David going into the TARDIS in 2009 and it said 'The Doctor's most faithful companion.'

After everything I've done in my career though, I'd have to say that my favourite role was in the theatre, when I played Nathan Detroit in Guys & Dolls."

RONNIE LE DREW
RAINBOW, PLAY DAYS

When puppeteers get a Harlequin award you're talking big league!– the puppet equivalent of the Oscars. Ronnie has had a distinguished career in film, theatre and TV bringing to life a host or weird and wonderful creatures along the way. Bill & Ben, Thunderbird puppets, meercats and a certain creature with a zip on his mouth to name but a few.

"I was born in Toronto, Canada and trained at the Little Angel Theatre, London under John Wright. My association with the Little Angel spans over thirty years as performer, and later as director.

Other theatre credits have included *Ala-al-din* (Clifford Heap Miniature Theatre UK Tour) *Through Wooden Eyes* (Hogarth Puppets UK Tour) *Han's the Bell Ringer* (Oxford Play House and Civic Theatre Darlington) *Angelo* (Purcell Room, London) *Soldiers Tale, The Box of Toys, Amahl and the Night Visitors, Genevieve De Brabant, Reynard the Fox.* (Queen Elizabeth Hall, London and Norwich Puppet Theatre.) *Cinderella, Frog Prince, Peter and the Wolf, Pinocchio,* (Midlands Arts Centre, Birmingham) and *Polynesia* in Doctor Dolittle UK Tour. Scottish Arts Council Funded Tours, and visits to America, Israel, Denmark, France, Belgium and Czechoslovakia followed.

Some of my numerous television credits begin in 1964 (I was a mere child) with *A Touch of Don Juan* for the BBC – narrated by Douglas Fairbanks JR. *The Little Mermaid* (Associated Re-diffusion) *Late Night line up, Mak the Sheep stealer, Michael Bentine's Potty Time, The Tommy Cooper Show* both for Thames TV. *Playdays, Mortimer and Arabel, Utterly Brilliant* with Timmy Mallet, *Good Morning with Anne and Nick, Jays World, Roger and the Rotten Trolls* and *Bills New Frock.*

I've also been fortunate to appear with Harry Corbett, Matthew Corbett and also with Richard Cadell on the *Sooty Show* and *Sooty Heights* mainly as Sweep, occasionally as Sooty and once as Scampy! However I'm probably best known as Zippy from *Rainbow* and later *Rainbow Days.* As Zippy, I've appeared

on *The Jim Davidson Show*, *The Generation Game*, Channel 5's *Night Fever*, *The Jonathan Ross Show*, *The World of Puppets*, *The Greatest 100 Kids TV Shows* as well as appearances at the Fridge, The Hammersmith Pallais, and numerous Universities, Night Clubs, and Discos all over Great Britain with the *Rainbow Disco Road Show* and *Rainbow's Play Your Cards Right*.

I've done my fair share of films too, including *The Naked Runner* which starred the late Frank Sinatra, *A Dandy in Aspic*, *Labyrinth*, *Muppet Christmas Carol*, *Muppet Treasure Island*, and *The Little Shop of Horrors*. Commercials include *Rowntree's Jelly Tots*, *Harvest Crunch*, *American Yellow Page's*, *London Docklands Crows* and even one for a Swedish toilet roll. And most recently Head puppeteer on the Brains Drench Water advert, I operated the Meerkat in the latest comparethemeerkat.com advert. One of the most enjoyable commercials I have worked on, would be for the Ideal Home Exhibition in the seventies, where I operated the original Bill and Ben...the flower pot men!

In August 2005 I became Muffin the Mule's Operator for all his appearances, TV and Theatre. Muffin is British Televisions first puppet icon. all I can say is....What an Honour! Also Look out for *Rainbow Live* the touring children's show with Zippy George and Bungle www.rainbowlive.co.uk

Recently pop videos have used puppets and what fun they are to work on.

I have taught at Little Angel Theatre, Central School of Speech and Drama, and founded The London School of Puppetry with my partner Caroline Astell-Burt. When time permits, I also perform my one man puppet shows for young children.

There's nothing I really do to prepare for being Zippy apart from reading the scripts. When I first joined the cast, I was able to watch the programme (it was transmitted five days a week at lunch times.) *Rainbow* started in 1972 and I joined in 1973 and remained till the very last episode.

When I was a new cast member I popped up and revealed myself on screen while the credits were still rolling. Thank goodness for recorded programmes. We did a short episode for the VTR people in which Geoffrey plays with his balls, Jane plays with her knockers....etc. This is now on YouTube and has become quite a famous clip. If you played it to pre-school children to day they would except it as a normal *Rainbow* programme. There was no swearing just a lot of double meanings if you get my drift.

THE INTELLIGENT FINANCE PUPPET

I didn't receive any advice for working in kids TV, I went into to it, as it were, at the deep end.....and as the years went by I became a better swimmer. Basically I learnt on the job. We all helped each other.

Of my favourite TV programmes, *Rainbow* must come first followed by Gerry Anderson's earlier programmes: *Four Feather Falls, Fireball XL5, Stingray, Thunderbirds* (by the way what fun it was operating Brains in the Drench advert) *Blue Peter, Magpie, Rubovia*, Oliver Postgate's programmes, *Paddington Bear*, Johnny Morris' programmes, *Bill and Ben* and *Muffin the Mule* and I am sure there are more...which have slipped my mind.

I'm most proud of my years at the Little Angel Theatre, the chance to work with the Henson company, *Rainbow* and working with the Corbett's on *Sooty and Sweep*, being Muffin the Mule's operator plus the UK tour of *Dr Dolittle* and having the chance to meet so many wonderful people in the entertainment business."

You can read more about Ronnie's work at his website www.ronnieledrew.com

PETER DUNCAN
BLUE PETER, DUNCAN DARES

I wouldn't want to engage Peter Duncan in a game of truth or dare! It's fair to say he has a bit of a daredevil reputation. Almost a pre-requisite for Blue Peter presenters today, Peter took it to another level and later starred in his own show. The former Chief Scout has done a great deal to revive the image of the scouts and received his very own gold Blue Peter badge in recognition of this.

"I began my career as an actor, and at 17, joined the National Theatre. I have walked the tightrope in the musical *Barnum*, played Bill Snibson in *Me and My Girl* and performed as Charlie Chaplin in *The Little Tramp*. In 1995 I was nominated for an Olivier award as Best Actor in a musical for my role in *The Card*. Over the last few years I've toured in Alan Ayckbourn's *Things we do for Love*, played the twins in *Corpse* and appeared as Stan Laurel in a production of *Laurel and Hardy* and recently took the role of Macduff in *Macbeth* and *Fantastic Mr Fox* at the Open Air Theatre in Regent's Park.

I became *Blue Peter's* 11th presenter in 1980 and on my first day I ended up cleaning the face of Big Ben. I worked alongside Simon Groom, Sarah Greene, Janet Ellis and Mark Curry during my two stints with the show. I guess I took over John Noakes' action man mantle – I completed the Royal Marines endurance course, became a circus acrobat, fought a Japanese sumo wrestler and ran the very first London marathon in under 3 hours.

After some complaints from viewers who thought my appearance was a bit scruffy they ran a competition to design me a new outfit and the winner was Darren Turner who designed the famous green and white checked suit.

I left *Blue Peter* in 1985 to make *Duncan Dares*, a series which capitalised on my adventurous side with stunts such as driving across the Irish Sea in a VW Beetle. In 2001 I directed a six part series called *Travel Bug* for CBBC in which me, my partner Annie and our four children backpacked our way around the world. In the two follow up series our journeys were shown in *Chinese Breakaway* and *Arthur's trip to India*.

I've worked as an actor and a presenter on TV on shows such as *The Childhood Friend, Sons and Lovers, Renoir My Father, Warship, Fathers and Families, Sam, Fallen Hero, King Cinder, Oranges and Lemons, The Flockton Flyer, Space 1999* and *The Big Race*. I've had parts in a few feature films, including

Stardust, Quilp, and a famous cameo in *Flash Gordon* where I met a rather gruesome end!

Some of my other recent TV credits include the 26 part slapstick comedy series *Demolition Dad* for Five and Channel 4's *The Games* – in which I took part as the oldest competitor ever. This year I've been supporting Red Nose Day with my dancing skills and I took my *Daft and Dangerous* show to the Edinburgh fringe during the summer.

I've appeared in *Faking it* as an Abba lookalike and I hold the dubious honour of being voted off first twice in *The Weakest Link*! I've often appeared in print and on news media defending and empowering the rights of young people on subjects such as teenage pregnancy, creativity and adventure lifestyle.

I've also had a long association with pantomime, following in my parent's footsteps, and has played many roles including Buttons, Peter Pan and Captain Hook, and through my own production company we've staged: *The Gingerbread Man, Erik The Viking, Robin Hood, Cinderella* and *Aladdin*. This Christmas I'm writing and directing *Jack and the Beanstalk* for the Oxford Playhouse.

From 2004 to 2009 I was made Volunteer Chief Scout of the United Kingdom who celebrated a hundred years of Scouting which included the world's largest jamboree where 40,000 young people attended from nearly every country on the planet.

I'm intending to carry on in public life, hoping to inspire young people with their creative aspirations to lead fulfilling and productive lives."

You can read more about Peter's career at his website www.heresoneimadeearlier.com

ANN EMERY
MRS MEAKER - RENTAGHOST

'Those crazy Meakers' took over the running of the Rentaghost business from the departed Mr. Mumford and that's when all the problems started! The Meakers — Harold with his moustache and hat and Ethel with her voice that could shatter glass! Ann is the sister of 70s comic Dick Emery and as a talented dancer she has gone on to further success.

"I was cast as Ethel Meaker by Jeremy Swan, producer of the series, and have enjoyed reasonable success since, in musicals and a variety of forms and other sorts, culminating in the role I have now, as Billy Elliot's 'Nana'. Long may the show continue."

You can see Ann in Billy Elliott at the Victoria Palace Theatre.

ANN (THIRD LEFT) WITH THE RENTAGHOST CAST

EMMA FORBES
GOING LIVE, LIVE & KICKING

Emma Forbes puts the mm into Emma! Saturday mornings were always worth getting up for. If her cooking didn't go quite accordingly to plan on *Going Live*, she certainly made up for it as the co-host of *Live and Kicking*.

"I got the job on Live and Kicking having been on *Going Live* as resident chef.....I only actually got onto *Going Live* in the first place by bombarding the Editor, Chris Bellinger, with letters and ideas...and very sweetly he would reply and we kept in contact until finally he gave me his time in a meeting. He asked me what else they could possibly do on the show, and I replied (literally off the top of my head) 'Cookery'. He gave me a 6 minute live slot the following Saturday and I had never done live TV, didn't meet Phillip til 3 mins before we went on air, and everything I made was a disaster...but it made people laugh!

So...when *Live and Kicking* came up for grabs I had done 3 years on *Going Live* but still had to do endless auditions before getting the role. It was, and is without doubt, the best job in telly and the best job I have ever ever had.

Every week was different. I loved every week and the funny memories are endless. I sang 'You're the One that I Want' live and John Barrowman laughed so much, as did Andi Peters, we could barely present due to the fact I was horrendous at singing!

The best advice I ever received for working in TV came from both the Editor of *Live and Kicking* and from Sarah Greene – both of whom told me to 'remember to breathe' – sounds stupid, but when you are nervous and live it's so difficult to remember to pause and breathe and if you don't you speak too fast!!

My own favourite kids TV programmes were Swap Shop, Magpie, Why don't you..?, Vision On and The Muppet Show. Quite a few basically!!"

EMMA FORBES

DEREK FOWLDS
MR. DEREK - BASIL BRUSH

In a long and distinguised career Derek has had more than just a brush with kids TV. From his partnership with Basil Brush to the walls of Westminster or policing the hills of Aidensfield, he's made the switch in a heartbeat!

Before I got to work with Basil, I'd been acting for 9 years in shows such as *Armchair Theatre*, *Z-Cars* and *Doctor Finlay's Casebook* on TV, *Race against Time* and *Spring Awakening* in the theatre and the flims *Doctor in Distress*, *Frankenstein Created Woman* and *Hotel Paradiso*. I went to the BBC one day to audition. I'd got a bad cold, and I was never going to work with a a puppet, but I met Basil, and totally believed in him. Initially I did one series with him then went to Exeter to play Hamlet to exorcise the experience! But, I came back and ended up doing 8 series in total and 2 Royal Command performances, and in those 5 years we became best mates.

When people ask me what it's like working with a puppet, my reply is that I've never worked with a puppet, but I have worked with a few foxes!

I'm 71 now, and I didn't see telly until I was 18. I worked alongside the late Paul Eddington in *Yes Minister* and *Yes Prime Minister* and when Paul was 18 he was playing Will Scarlett in *Robin Hood* and I'd tease him about it, saying 'I remember watching you as a kid.'

The first thing I saw on TV was the Queen's Coronation in 1953, (the year I left school). There was only one TV in the street and everyone gathered round in one house. Before TV we would play outside kicking a ball around or playing cricket. It wasn't until I came home from National Service that mum said we had our own TV and I would watch *William Tell*.

Looking back on my career, there are a few things I'm most proud of. During my 50 years as an actor I've appeared in 13 plays in the West End, I've been on Broadway in *Chips and Everything* and of course working with Nigel Hawthorne and Paul Eddington in *Yes Minister* and *Yes Prime Minister* was a highlight. The one unfortunate thing is that I've not had any of Anthony Hopkin's parts yet!"

DEREK GRIFFITHS
PLAY SCHOOL, PLAYAWAY, SUPER TED

Is there anything that Derek hasn't done? Actor, musician, singer, and wibbly-wobbly jelly-on-a-plate impressionist. Derek is certainly up there with the greats of kids TV. If it's not singing and composing theme tunes, then it's presenting, or voicing teddy bears with super powers!

"I was doing a panto at Greenwich Theatre and Miranda Connell, who was a presenter on *Play School*, saw me and came to see me backstage, and said 'I'm going to tell them all at the Beeb about you', and they got me in for an audition.

I never thought I was suitable for *Play School*, I was beating up members of the audience in the show. I kept saying to them that I wasn't the right guy for this, and it took some persuading before they took me on.

However, after I did start, I felt I wanted to change the concept of music offered to children. What they had seemed awful and archaic and I wanted to get some jazz musicians in. It took a bit of doing, but it was justified when we started to get letters saying 'Can we have more music from Derek?'

There was lots of innuendo and naughty stuff in the studio. I was doing a piece to camera, then the camera moved onto my co-presenter, and while the camera was on her I got a message that the camera was coming back onto me, and I had 3 minutes to ad lib something! 3 minutes is a long time on TV, especially if you've not rehearsed anything and without any warning.

They plonked a lump of plasticine in front of me and the camera came back on to me, so I said 'Right, this is a guessing game' and I started to roll out the plasticine into a long sausage shape. 'Can you guess what it is?' I continued to roll it out and it became more and more phallic. I then stood it on its end!

By this time, the camera crew had locked the cameras and were in the corner absolutely wetting themselves laughing. The plasticine then started to lean over! As the 3 minutes came to an end I simply said 'That was Nelson's Column. Good bye!'

As well as the kids, a lot of the audience were made up of policemen, chefs and shift workers, and if they bumped into me they said 'How did you get away with that?!?'

Another time they wanted to do a 'bathing the baby' piece. They asked me to do it at first and I thought the female presenter should do that and I wanted to do something with more meat to it, but it came back to me, so I thought 'I'll show them' and in the lunch break I got a felt tip pen and drew pubes on Hamble.

I started doing my piece to camera. 'This may be your baby brother or sister.' The doll was sitting on a draining board with its back to the camera as I washed her, and at the very last moment I turned her round and opened her legs! There were screams! The director was shouting 'CUT! CUT!' I'd never heard them say that before! They asked me if I knew anything about it, by this time it had begun to wash off, and I just said 'Oh!!! Who did that..?? That's terrible...!!' I was never asked to do it again!

Narrating *Super Ted* was such an event. It was with all the old mates, Jon Pertwee, Melvyn Hayes, Roy Kinnear, Victor Spinetti and Sheila Steafel. It was such a laugh, so much so that they brought in a film documentary crew to produce a 'making of' programme but the couldn't use it as it was just so filthy!

I think the highlight of my career was getting the freedom, after *Play School*, to create documentaries for children. I did one called the *Flying Documentary* where I put a camera in the front seat of a plane to show to children that it's not some mystical thing and that they can be part of it.

I used to get a log of negative comments saying 'You'll never make it' even school reports were discouraging. I was at Swansea university doing a late night review at the Edinburgh Festival and I went to the bar afterwards and a guy said to me 'You'll never get anywhere, you're the wrong colour!' I'd love to meet him now!"

DEREK GRIFFITHS

ATALANTA HARMSWORTH
ANIMAL KWACKERS, POTAMUS PARK

"Rory, Rory, tell us a story..." Well this story is about a dog, a tiger, a lion and a monkey. Bongo, Rory, Twang and Boots – the large-headed, four-piece, animal rock and roll group called *Animal Kwackers* who arrived onto our TV screens in a space ship! What was even more amazing was the realisation after years and years that Bongo was actually, at one time, played by a girl! Bongo, Bongo tell us <u>your</u> story...

I remember sitting on the floor watching television when the first ever episode of *Animal Kwackers* was shown. I was still at school and the programme was rather too young for me – but little did I know that I'd end up playing one of the characters in the show!!

I moved to London from Sussex when I left school, in order to study drama in Holborn. I very quickly got a job as a session singer and voice over artist in an East London Recording studio, and was asked by the boss there if I could play drums. I am a Musician's Union member and so I took up the challenge. I joined right at the end but it was great fun and we went on to tour *Animal Kwackers* at all the major theatre venues around England during childrens holidays. We did our own warm-up when we toured, which was a luminous puppet show. One time 'Twang' (the monkey) was fooling about on stage and fell off, knocking himself out temporarily. John Bassett (who played 'Boots') immediately got on the tannoy and asked if there was a vet in the house!

I was the 'baby' of the group and I went onto marry Step Morley who played 'Twang'. We were in several bands together. Firstly as a three piece

BACKSTAGE ON ANIMAL KWACKERS

POTAMUS PARK

with Bev Doyle (who had played 'Rory') and then in various bands with influences from rock to blues to reggae. Our time together had started in a recording studio; moved on to 'animal passion' in the TV show and, unfortunately, ended up in divorce seven years later.

I pursued acting and went back to drama school to get a proper training. I have been lucky and worked in many diverse roles in theatre, television and voice-overs. I was asked to play another skin role for Carlton Television's *Potamus Park*. I played 'Hippy', a rather chaotic and bossy Mum, in the show which was shot at Pinewood Studios. The show ran for three years and in the final year I was pregnant, and didn't dare tell anyone in case it would threaten my job. I did have to let my dresser Jemima Cotter know, however, as she had to keep letting my costume out.

My son, Alfred Harmsworth, is now eleven years old and as I always took him on set with me when I was working at Pinewood Studios on *Potamus Park*, from an early age he would believe that anything was possible - having spent so much of his early years being surrounded by fake snow and colourful sets, believing that all things could fly (with the help of pulleys) and that creatures such as moles and sunflowers spoke to him (we had *Sesame Street* puppeteers working on our show). He has now been acting since he was four and a half years old, appearing in films with Jim Broadbent and Forest Whitaker amongst others. Alfred is in *Bright Star* by Jane Campion coming out in 2009, and we have been in several television advertisements and dramas together and I am very proud of him.

I grew up with *Watch with Mother* and *Jackanory*. My favourites were *The Clangers*, *The Herbs* (little remembered) and *Roobarb and Custard*.

Skin-work is much harder than it looks but above all, in all the childrens shows that I've been involved in, I've been lucky enough to have had a wonderful time laughing a lot, having fun and working with terrifically creative and imaginative people. That can't be bad for a day job!"

FRED HARRIS
PLAY SCHOOL, RAGTIME, CHOCK-A-BLOCK

Fred was one of my favourite presenters. Always fun and lively, his sense of enjoyment really stuck in my memory. I also shared the same interest in maths, science and computers. From square windows to BBC Micro computers and giant calculators, plus the occasional run-in with the *Play School* toys, Fred is definitely my favourite chock-a-bloke. What follows is a transcript of a recorded conversation.

"In the early 1970s I was helping to run a budget theatre company down in Southampton. We'd met at college in Coventry – I'd been doing a Post Grad teaching diploma there. I originally graduated in Maths, but decided I wanted to do something in drama. The only job I could get at the time was a Maths teaching job. Then these mates of mine rescued me from teaching, and asked if I would like to starve in a theatre company, earning next to no money, and I said 'Yeah, why not!' So we moved down to Southampton. We were a band of actors called Chameleon, and we used to work at colleges, schools and did street theatre. It was an exciting thing to do, but there was no money in it. We were living on lentils and beans with obvious results. My duvet hardly touched the mattress at night! So various members of the band would take jobs that came their way to make ends meet. I used to do the odd shift at BBC Radio Solent for very little money, but just enough to buy a bag of crisps occasionally. I would go around with a tape recorder doing interviews and I hosted a kids phone-in programme on a Saturday and I also used to write a little drama for them. One of the DJ's down there asked me if I'd ever thought about doing anything on television, and I said no because I thought it would be a case of who you know, but he said not necessarily. He said 'What do you imagine yourself doing? What would you really like to do?'

FRED ON RAGTIME

When I'd been teaching, I used to come home at 4 o'clock, in the days when you didn't have to run clubs and so on afterwards, and as I was coming out of school there was a Radio Rentals shop window and I was always going past when *Play School* was on. I'd not seen this show before and didn't know what it was about. There were about 17 or 18 TV sets all showing Derek Griffiths, looning about, being a frog or whatever, and wondered what the hell that was. One week I was off sick with flu, and I put the telly on at about 4 o'clock and there was Derek Griffiths again doing his stuff, and I just fell in love with the programme. I thought it was brilliant programming, it knew exactly what it was doing. So I said to the DJ I wouldn't mind presenting a programme like *Play School*, it's got a lot of integrity, so he said what I should do is write to the last name on the credits, which in those days was Cynthia Felgate, the Executive Producer. So I wrote to her saying I think I can do that programme, and I got a letter back saying thank you for your application, we'll put you on file, and let you know if anything crops up.

About 6 months went by and I didn't hear any more so I thought that's the end of that one. Then I got a letter from Cynthia asking if I could come up to London to do an audition, but it was for the following Tuesday. I was booked into a school with the theatre company so I had to find someone to cover for me, and I came up and did this 'outside audition'. They saw about 60 people during the course of the day, and they shortlisted me, which was very nice, and they sent me a script for an audition that would actually be in the television studio. At that stage I'd never even seen a television studio before and I was absolutely shit scared. I was terrified. I prepared a couple of items with sock puppets, and went in to rehearse my audition and made a total pig's ear of it. It was just a dummy run at that stage and wasn't recorded. The producer, who was doing the auditions, would have a chat with us in the green room and gave me some notes, and I now know that the purpose of that was to see how well I took the notes. She took me outside, and instead of saying you were absolute rubbish, which I was, she was very enthusiastic,and said don't worry about that, be yourself, do it this way etc, and on my way back in she squeezed me by the arm and said "Look Fred, don't let me down, my money's on you." and that was the most important thing she could have said, because I went in there and felt supremely confident – all because someone had said "my money's on you".

I can remember that audition pretty well. I had some sock puppets, and said 'all you need for this is an old sock' and I pulled a sock out of a bag, but unfortunately it wasn't the one that matched the puppet that I'd made, so I'd obviously picked up the wrong sock. Earlier in the day I would have gone to pieces, but because I felt quite confident, I had to get rid of that sock and pick up the right one. So I sniffed it, and said 'Ohh, preferably a clean one', threw it over my shoulder and picked out the sock I really wanted. One of the cameramen was giggling audibly on the recording at that, and I think that, as much as anything, got me the job. So it was a bit of luck and a bit of advice that helped me get the job on *Play School* and, I suppose, having seen Derek doing his stuff, because Derek was brilliant and I still think he is.

In a sense it was a conscious decision to move into childrens' television, although the work I was doing with the theatre company was for children and adults as well, and since *Play School* I've done heaps of adult telly anyway. I don't see a huge difference, personally, between working for children and adults, you just have to keep the language simple. The basic rules of communication are the same. You should never talk down to a child. He or she might be as bright as you are or even brighter. They just haven't lived very long!

One of the things that working in children's telly taught me, which is really useful for doing adult telly as well, is that you've got to be more interesting than the other things around the viewer who's watching. It was an overriding principle on *Play School* that the children weren't obliged to sit and watch you, no one chained them down, so you had to make them <u>want</u> to watch you. I always used to imagine there was a child out there, sitting in his room at home, surrounded by colourful toys, that were all vying for his attention, and I had to be more attention grabbing than those toys. That was a thought I kept in my head whenever I was working in children's television, but the same thing applies to adults as well. Ok, they're not surrounded by toys, but they have chores to do around the house or shopping lists and all kinds of things. If you're doing a programme for an adult you've still got to be more interesting than the other things that he or she could be doing with their time. So I think there's a lot of overlap between the two.

The great thing about *Play School* was that people were there because they wanted to be there. They were committed. I'm talking about the presenters, writers, producers, everybody. Nobody was treating it as a 'stepping stone' to somewhere else. We all got very annoyed if someone suggested that children's programmes were 'easy' or 'second best'. On the contrary, kids are very discerning and difficult to please.

I'm not sure if it's easier working with humans or soft toys. Soft toys don't answer back, but they don't always sit up straight. There's an outtake where I beat up Big Ted which was on *Auntie's Bloomers* and various other clip shows.

When we were filming *Play School*, you had to keep to time, you couldn't overrun as it was shot as if it was live, even though you could do pick up shots later if you needed to. On one occasion I was doing a little song with the toys sat in front of me, and every time I went round the song had to count off one of the toys, and, for some reason, every time I came to Big Ted he fell over. Of course, you ad lib and carry on as if nothing's gone wrong and you make something of it. I would say 'Oh come on Big Ted, sit up, stop messing about'. The next time it happens I'd say 'I don't know what's wrong with him today, he keeps falling over' and the third time I'd say 'Now come on, behave your self Ted'. But every time I did this it was adding to the length of the song, and eventually I got a cut-throat sign from the Floor Manager because the song was overrunning by a minute, which was a precious minute. So, believing that they'd stopped the tape, I then threw a tantrum and started hitting the teddy bears. I shouted 'I don't know why I work with these amateurs, I'm an artiste, for god's sake!' That's the kind of thing you do in the studio to keep up the spirits of the poor old cameraman who were doing the same thing every day of the week. What I didn't realise was that they were still recording at that stage, so that little bit of video tape escaped. But in a funny kind of way its earned me more money than any television programme ever had, because its been shown again and again on these outtake programmes. Every time they show it my agent manages to negotiate a little extra fee for it, so in all, its been shown about 30 or 40 times, and its added up to about £1500 I think, so I'm very glad that happened!

Of course all the *Play School* toys were divas off stage. There was Big Ted who did all his misbehaving, but I think he was only doing that as a bit of charity work so I could earn a bit of extra money on the outtakes!

We always felt the *Play School* toys had their own personalities. I used to love Little Ted, partly because you could animate him very easily. For example, if you were holding him in one hand, you could put one finger either side of his arm, and as you're saying goodbye, you could be waving with your left arm, and with Ted in your right hand, you could make his arm wave just by wiggling your fingers. It made him look as though he was alive, which was quite a nice little touch.

Hamble was just as hated by the presenters as she was by the viewers, but she was even more hated by the crew who would regularly string her up by the neck with a piece of rope, the only trouble was that Hamble was the only toy that was irreplaceable. There were spare Teds and Humpties, but only one Hamble.

I'm told that Hamble had belonged to Cynthia Felgate when she was a girl, and was a Woolworth's doll from the late 1940s/early 50s. She wasn't a china doll, but was made of rubber, and most of these rubber dolls had rotted over the years, so there was just Hamble, and one other owned by a woman in Cheshire. She had, allegedly, been offered a fortune to sell her doll to *Play School*, but she wouldn't do it because every time they had to send Hamble to the dolls hospital, she would hire her version of Hamble to *Play School* for a couple of hundred quid, so she was quids in every time she did this.

Hamble was pretty gruesome I have to say! I had to do an item with Hamble, where I had to undress her and give her a bath. We would do a stagger through, where each shot is lined up, then do a run through which you'd try to do in real time, and they'd put a stop watch on it and see how the item's running, then you'd have a break then do the recording. The run through had gone pretty well, and I took a break as it was now lunchtime. When I came back to do the recording, one of the crew had, shall I say, adapted Hamble's body slightly using a felt-tip pen! This was on the take and there I was, undressing Hamble, and when I got down to her knickers, and pulled her drawers down, she suddenly sprouted pubic hair, which I have to say, totally corpsed me. But we had a bit of a problem as this was the recording, and we didn't have the deputy Hamble. Somebody thought I'd done it, but I honestly didn't do it. One of the backstage people had to go away and try to scrub Hamble clean while we recorded the rest of the programme, and did that bit as an insert to be put in later. I'm not saying heads rolled, but it was a good gag, but something that should be done on the run through and not on the recording!

I got on with lots of my co-presenters. There are some I really looked forward to 'playing' with, because that's what it felt like. Toni Arthur was fun, Carol Chell was great, I love Carol Chell. I'd use to try and make Carol corpse and I could never ever mange it. One occasion I was being a milkman and Carol was coming to the door. There were four different doors and she would come to each one as a different character, and she had to come out and ask 'Have you got any yoghurts?' I would say 'Oh yes, I've got strawberry or vanilla, which do you fancy?', 'Oh strawberry please...' etc. On the take I decided, just for a bit of spice, to say 'We're trying out some new flavours today madam, we've got cheese & onion or liver & bacon'. I was hoping to crack a smile, but she wouldn't corpse, she was so professional – she was great fun also – but she kept a totally straight face. She looked me straight in the eyes and said 'Ooh liver and bacon sounds interesting' at which point I just collapsed as she said it so nicely. It went out like that, and I'm sure the kids were wondering what on earth Fred was laughing about.

Carol Leader was great fun, I worked with Carol on another programme on the radio. I used to love working with her, and it was brilliant working with Chloe Ashcroft, we always got each other giggling. The production team didn't mind this, as long as it didn't exclude the viewer.

ON LOCATION WITH CAROL LEADER AND A FARMER

Something that really challenged my professionalism was when we were doing a programme about mini beasts. The programme started with me kneeling at some blocks at the front of a garden set up, in a huge tray, filled with earth, plants and rocks, and it's supposed to be covered with creepy crawlies; ants, spiders, bugs, beetles and worms. On the run through and the stagger through, when the camera looked down for the creepy crawlies, they were all hiding because the studio lights were so hot and they wanted to get in the dark. The producer told the Floor Manager and Assistant Floor Manager to get as many bug and beetles and snails during lunch, and sent them to the Blue Peter Garden to get dozens of them because he wanted the place to be crawling with them when the camera zooms in.

They came back with absolutely hundreds of them, and they put them onto this earth tray, covered it with a tarpaulin so they felt secure and in the dark, and we went for the take. So here am I, kneeling by these blocks, and the Floor Manager counts down, and with about 5 seconds to go they ripped off this tarpaulin so all these bugs are visible, and the first thing the bugs do is try and find somewhere dark. They'd taken away most of the foliage and the rocks so they couldn't hide anywhere, so the only thing these bugs could do was jump over the side of the block and look for the nearest dark cave. Well, the nearest dark cave was Fred's trousers! So within seconds I literally had dozens of spiders, beetles and creepy crawlies of all sorts climbing up as far as they could into these flared jeans of mine for security.

So here am I, talking to the camera now, I'd just said hello to the viewers, and all these creepy crawlies were crawling around inside my trousers and trying to carry on as I would normally. It was a real test of my professionalism but I think I pulled it off, but I certainly felt like having a shower after that!

I can't really remember many of the programmes I used to watch when I was a child, we didn't have a telly until quite late on, but I do remember one programme in the mid 50s with Rolf Harris called *Whirlygig*, with Humphrey Lestock, and a puppet called Mr. Turnip. I don't suppose many people can remember that one! There was another one called *Billy Bean and his Funny Machine* which was a puppet show. *Rag Tag and Bobtail*, *Bill & Ben* and *Pugwash* was very good. I was delighted later to meet Peter Hawkins the guy who did the voices of all the *Pugwash* people. He was one of my idols, because I always liked character voices, and he was brilliant.

What am I most proud of? I take pride in doing a good job at work and I like to think I go that extra mile, so I will spend a ridiculous amount of time learning the lines if I have to. I love working in a team and I don't particularly like being the number one guy, even though in a lot of my career I've had to be the only presenter in certain programmes. Sometimes I've been the presenter, writer and sometimes the deviser. I like doing all of those things, but I far prefer working in a team. It goes back to the theatre group. That was a really nice way of working. A few years ago the BBC were running out of money, and I had to write and front a radio programme I used to do. But this time they handed me a tape recorder and said 'bring us back a series' and I had to be the deviser, presenter, writer, sound recordist and tape editor even. I can do that sort of thing but I much prefer to have a cross fertilisation of ideas from other people.

I could be described as 'the award losing Fred Harris', which is a funny thing to be proud of. *Ragtime* got a BAFTA, it was called the SFTA in those days (Society of Film & Television Arts). It was the same organisation but they've just rebranded themselves since. In 1973 we got the BAFTA for the best children's programme of the year. I'd only just come into children's television so I thought this was amazing, and thought was it really that easy to win a BAFTA? The next chance I got of a BAFTA was in 1980, when for some peculiar reason 4 different programmes that I was involved in had all been nominated. Two were nominated for the best Education programme, a numeracy programme for Yorkshire Television called *Counting On*, and schools maths programme for Central Television called *Basic Maths*, and the BBC, for some reason, had decided to nominate *Play School* and they'd chosen one of the programmes I was in. London Weekend Television nominated a comedy programme (really for adults) called *End of Part One* which was broadcast in the family/children's slot. All four of these programmes were nominated for the BAFTA Harlequin award which had two guises, one was for the best children's entertainment programme and one for the best education programme. The poor judges had to sit through 4 different programmes with Fred Harris in them, and they must have been sick to the back teeth of seeing me, so it's no wonder none of them won, but the upshot was that I lost 4 BAFTA's in 2 minutes, which is quite an achievement I think, so that's something I can be truly proud of!"

FRED HARRIS

PHILLIP HODSON FRSA
GOING LIVE AGONY UNCLE

If you had a problem, there was only one person to talk to. Not your mum, or your nan, it was the Saturday morning agony uncle Phillip Hodson. Dispenser of invaluable advice to youngsters for many years, and one of the unsung hereos of kids TV.

"I got into children's TV when the producer of *Saturday Superstore* (later *Going Live!*) Cathy Gilbey phoned me to say she was impressed by my radio show's high profile amongst teenagers (late nights in London) and would I bring this audience to the box?

The only advice I got about doing the job was to 'be yourself'. I realised that television is normal life with cameras in the corners – but a camera has a name and it's 'YOU'. I loved the medium from the start.

My advice didn't really change at all during six years on the programmes but the shows got much braver about the types of issues we could tackle – in a nutshell, we went from talking about acne and fear of the dark to talking about the anguish of bereavement and the vileness of sexual abuse. I am proud that we rescued several children from the most horrible home situations – our most difficult call was made off air – having to tell a mum, whose uncle abused her, that he was doing the same thing to her daughter who'd written in for help.

There was one time when I spent 20 minutes alone with Maggie Thatcher in the Green Room when we were both on the pop quiz – all grey eyes and chat about her daughter's difficult romantic experiences with a Tory MP (Jonathan Aitken). Friends accused me of NOT having the guts to mount an assassination! On another occasion, the Canadian comic Mike McShane once pretended I was his long lost brother because we shared the identical pattern of male baldness.

My girlfriend wanted us to make love in the dressing room but I assure you this never happened!

I got a letter addressed to 'Dear Acne Uncle' - and many kids called me an agony 'aunt'. I still bump into 20- and 30-somethings today who suddenly say things like "Ohmigod weren't you on Going Live! - I watched you all the time when I was 7". Makes you feel forever young!

My favourite children's tv as a kid was *Blue Peter* (I won a competition and got a set of stamps from Mauritius - still have them if anyone wants to buy 'em!). I thought *Muffin the Mule* was naff, *Andy Pandy* was in serious need of therapy and *Bill and Ben* were a little introverted. (Their flower-bedmate friend 'Weed' seemed more attractively subversive). I sensed the *Lone Ranger* rode a speeded up horse that would have died of heart failure and *Hopalong Cassidy* was clearly the love child of President Eisenhower and a rabbit!

If you're still in need of advice you can get in touch with Phillip through his website www.philliphodson.co.uk

PHILLIP HODSON

ANNA HOME OBE

FORMER BBC HEAD OF CHILDREN'S PROGRAMMES

Chief Executive of the Children's Film and Television Foundation, a Trustee of the Prince of Wales' Foundation for Children and the Arts (CATA) and Chair of the Showcomotion Children's Media Conference plus a BAFTA lifetime achievement award recipient, Anna has had a long and distinguished career in children's television. A former Head of Children's programmes at the BBC she was responsible for all children's output. She revived the Sunday teatime classic dramas and one of her last decisions before retiring was to commission *Teletubbies*.

"I started in children's television in 1964 where I worked as a researcher, then Director, Producer and Executive Producer latterly specialising in Children's Drama. I started *Grange Hill*, the controversial school series and during the 80s I worked at TVS as Deputy Director of Programmes.

I wanted to work in childrens television because I wanted to do something educational but not too educational and I loved children's books and stories. I used to listen to *Children's Hour* on the radio when I was a child, especially the serials; and the comedians, on radio and in the music halls used to entertain me as well as pantomimes and summer shows. There wasn't any tele!!

I think the secret to making a great children's programme is understanding the audience and telling a good story in whatever genre.

There is a great deal more children's programming these days but that has not meant a great deal more choice; there is a lack of long form drama and factual programming and there is too little which is challenging or demanding. Save Kid's TV which I chair is campaigning for more of this kind of material in the digital world. Sadly it probably requires Government intervention both in terms of regulation and funding

The one particular thing I'm most proud of is fighting for the audience to be taken seriously and programmes to be funded properly."

Currently Anna is Chair of the Save Kids TV campaign which is actively campaigning for a new online and broadcast service for children – with adequate funding to provide high-quality, UK-produced drama, factual and entertainment content missing from broadcast schedules and websites. Further details can be found at www.savekidstv.org.uk I hope you can lend your support.

VICKY IRELAND MBE
YOU & ME, WORDS & PICTURES

Words and Pictures' teaching methods included the use of books, songs, picture stories and a magic pencil which drew the letters – 'Down to the bottom, up and round'. In the late 80's Vicky Ireland and the loud, mildly disruptive cartoon character Charley presented *Words and Pictures* in a library set up with real children as live pupils. Vicky made a record 84 appearances fronting the show, and her work with children throughout her career has been recognised with an MBE.

"I was raised in a family friendly hotel in Scarborough, attended he Central School of Speech and Drama and was the youngest member of the first TIE (Theatre in Education) tean at the Belgrade Theatre Coventry. I then acted in various reps including the Theatre Royal York and as luck had it, the TV producer, Frank Kilbride, saw me play the Wicked Fairy in the pantomime and invited me to work for Yorkshire Television. This was the start of various presenting jobs in children's television including *Mr. Trimble*, *You and the World*, *Stepping Stones*, *Me and You* and *Words and Pictures*.

Words and Pictures for BBC TV was very special to me and I worked on it for twelve years. This fitted in brilliantly with being a young mum and having two small children in tow as the Producer, Moyra Gambleton, was very sympathetic and allowed me to occasionally bring them with me and for them to appear with the other children in the show.

Moyra, a skilled and dedicated producer, had a comprehensive background in education and every aspect of the show was conceived and carried out with loving care. Its objective was to use story-telling, images, pictures and a cartoon character to encourage children to learn to both read and write, and was seen up and down the country by thousands of children and their teachers. I always felt huge pride to be part of the team that made the programme and it was great fun going from London to the BBC studio in White Ladies Road, Bristol where one was always treated with kindness and respect. A wonderful job where I felt happy and fulfilled.

CHARLEY

The show was nominated for a BAFTA, and although it didn't win, it was very rewarding that the skill and care surrounding the show was recognised. Episodes have since been seen all around the world and I feel honoured that cartoon Charley and I have helped so many children along the road to a lifelong enjoyment of words and pictures.

As well as appearing on TV I have occasionally written for it; episodes of *Pipkins* for ATV and *The Ark* for Granada, then two series of *Happy Families*, based on the books by Allan Ahlberg for BBC TV, which were nominated for a GB Writer's Guild Award.

After leaving *Words and Pictures* I became Artistic Director of Polka Theatre in London, a family friendly theatre with huge similarities to the hotel I was raised in, and where I spent fourteen very happy years commissioning, producing, writing and directing plays for children as well as making sure the building was exciting to visit.

Most recently I have adapted and directed six books by the author Jacqueline Wilson which have toured the UK. I have also worked with other wonderful authors such as Phillip Pullman, Michael Morpurgo, Malorie Blackman and Lynne Reid Banks and with the best children's dramatists including Charles Way and Mike Kenny.

I have 10 published plays for children and have ongoing commissions for various companies. Along with the actress Kumiko Mendl, I am Co-Artistic Director of the theatre company 'A Thousand Cranes'.

The rest of my time is devoted to being a board member of TYA-UK (Theatre for Young Audiences, UK) and Vice Chair of ACA (Action for Children's Arts) – two charities about which I care passionately, both concerned with the place and importance of the arts in the lives of children and the respect of childhood.

IN THE STUDIO

MOYRA GAMBLETON & VICKY

In 2002 I was awarded an MBE for services to children's drama, the first of its kind and in 2008 I was elected a Fellow of the Royal Society for the Arts.

My career could not have happened without the devoted support of my husband, the actor John Rowe, and my two children, Olly and Annie.

I loved my time in Children's TV and have many happy memories. Here's luck and love to all those of you working in it now and all those yet to come. I wish Garry and his book every success."

You can keep up to date with Vicky's latest work at her official website www.vickyireland.com

MAT IRVINE
SWAP SHOP, SATURDAY SUPERSTORE

If one man has done his bit for recycling then it has to be Mat Irvine. Famed for making space ships out of every day appliances, he was responsible for cereal boxes in our house disappearing before all the contents were consumed! Mat became the face of the BBC's Special Effects department, but Mat's remit extended beyond just model making. Mat talks about his career so far and reveals the truth behind a long standing urban myth about a certain metallic dog!

"Building models was what most boys did in the sixties as there was little else to do until you discovered girls and cars, (not necessarily in that order...). Probably most sensible boys then concentrated on the latter, but some - including me - continued with the former, (er, as well as the latter...).

My first job with the BBC was in the photograph library for Television News, still at that time located at Alexandra Palace in North London. However when TV News moved to Television Centre, (the early 1970s), we joined forces with an existing photo library. The head of that other unit was Hazel Gill, who's sister was Rosemary Gill – at that time Assistant Editor on *Blue Peter.*

Later I had moved to the Visual Effects Department, and Rosemary created *Swap Shop - Multi-Coloured Swap Shop* to give it its full, though rarely used, title. For some reason, (and to this day I don't know why), she remembered I'd moved to FX and asked me to appear on, what transpired to be, the second programme. A few weeks later they asked me again, and I think I said something along the lines of, "Well I've done it, why not use someone else?", and they said, "Well they (the viewers) know you now...", which I suppose is a fair point.

Many probably think we worked on programmes such as *Doctor Who* all the time, but although this was of course very important, in many ways it was a small part of FX work. Overall we probably did far more work for the Light Entertainment and Children's Departments.

Some of the largest, and most time-consuming effects, are the physical of 'floor' effects, such as adding rain to a scene. I recall once telling a production to add a note to the paperwork along the lines of warning everyone to dress up nice and dry as 'FX rain was wetter than normal rain' – based on the fact that there would be much more of it – just so it would show up on camera! (They laughed – but it must have sunk in as I saw it printed very prominently on the top of the filming schedule!)

But at the other end of the scale we could be lighting a log fire in a grate in a stately home. One instance was at Leeds Castle in Kent for one of the Shakespeare dramas, (the little-known *Henry VIII*). And it is an 'effect', (besides the chimney being blocked so you couldn't light a 'real' fire anyway), as the fire had to be constant for continuity, so the flames were from a bottled gas supply and logs had to be fake so they didn't burn away. We did things like that that no one else did a great deal of the time - the more obvious effects such as miniatures, crashes and explosions were only a part of the whole story.

To wreck a popular urban myth, no I didn't 'build' in the sense of 'design', K9 in *Doctor Who* - that was my colleague Tony Harding. I didn't actually have anything to do with 'him' at that point, though I did work on that *Doctor Who* story, 'The Invisible Enemy' — mind you so did most of the Department, as it was a very 'effects heavy' show. Very soon however I had a hand — or more likely a spanner — in him, as I was one of the few in the Department that knew anything even vaguely about radio control at that time. (Oddly this was still very much in its infancy, even in 1977!) But since then I got involved in redesigning the mechanics and radio control systems, and it sort of grew.

Most of my time on the original series of *Doctor Who*'s was with Tom Baker. He was fun to work with, but had his moments like most people and had a very lugubrious sense of humour!

The reappearance of K-9 in the new *Doctor Who* and the story 'School Reunion', was a complete surprise as he was very much a child (or rather dog) of the 1970s and 80s. I was also slightly surprised they didn't want him redesigned, but it then transpired that this story was a continuation of the story I'd worked on in 1981, 'K-9 & Company'.

The 'rusty K-9', constructed out of the original lightweight K-9 body, had a fake 'futuristic' interior, and underneath was running on modified radio control car mechanics. However the K-9, that the Doctor 'sent back to Sarah-Jane' in the closing scene of that episode, was the original. Perhaps ironically it could cope far better with rougher surfaces than the 'newer Dog', as I had redesigned it all those years ago so that he could keep up with Tom Baker striding off down the road.

These days separate companies do all the different types of effects. In the 'old days' we did it all and no-one really specialised in one particular thing. However in the 1980s the BBC started to shut down the servicing departments on the theory that those who got the programmes made could get it done cheaper if it was sourced from outside companies. The producers could choose to spend the money where they wanted to, though this can loose the integrity of the programme a bit. It also bought up some strange situations such as despite them owning their own studio space some programmes would go elsewhere and pay for other studios, so although it possibly made sense on paper, in reality the system was paying again.

I left the BBC in 1993 and I moved more into production; the odd bit of directing and the like. I had a few goes at setting up a movie, (which is harder than working for the BBC!), and spread myself around doing a bit of museum design on the one hand and being one of creators of Robot Wars on the other.

As I don't really do 'effects' on a day-to-day overall CGI doesn't actually have any impact. However it is a misconception to think that it is 'all CGI' these days. Yes a lot is, but miniatures are still used a great deal - even if it is 'only' to then scan them into the computer for CGI. CGI is another tool to use - but like many tools (he says glibly) if you use it wrong you can hurt yourself!

I did, infamously, give away one secret of model making, and people always remind me about it. We needed a spacecraft for Season Two of *Blake's 7*, just something to appear on Zen's screen for a couple of seconds. A company like Lucas's Industrial Light and Magic would probably take six months to create something but we didn't have the time - or money - so we needed something quicker. However as I was directing the model filming, I could choose how it would be shot, and ended up diving down a box of scrap plastic parts, (likely got from the Proops warehouse in Edgware Road - a source for many a part), emerging with the casings for two Morphy Richard hairdryers. The basics for this craft were the two hairdryers stuck together though I maintain if I hadn't given away the secret on Swap Shop no-one would ever have known!

In general the Visual Effects Department received many letters, most along the lines of, 'How can I get into special effects'. As I'd been seen on screen, I tended to get more letters than others, (though I hesitate to use the term 'fan mail'!). I did try to reply to these as it was good PR for me as well as the BBC. I still get people saying to me 'I used to watch you on TV and you prompted me to get into the business...' I've recently finished filming for *The Sarah-Jane Adventures* and not one, but two, other FX guys said they'd written to me when they were much younger! (And I'd obviously replied.) Others who apparently also saw my much earlier efforts on such as *Swap Shop* and *Super Store* were the impressionist John Culshaw, the actor and writer Mark Gatiss, and a Doctor by the name of David Tennant.

Mat and Mike Tucker are writing a book about the BBC FX Department, which is due to be published for Christmas 2010.

SIR DEREK JACOBI CBE
DOCTOR WHO, IN THE NIGHT GARDEN

Sir Derek Jacobi, in my opinion, is a contender for future legend, a future-kind, so to speak! Not only was his portrayal of Professor Yana/The Master in the *Doctor Who* episode *Utopia* so memorable, but he has added to his status with his narration for *In the Night Garden* which, I believe, is going to be a future classic. After all, everyone enjoys a great big ponk! In the money-orientated world of kids TV these days, this programme has all the charm of the classic shows of the 70s. But what attracted this great Shakespearean actor to the world of Iggle Piggle?

"As a jobbing actor I respond to offers of work that offer originality and fun, and I enjoy working in a recording studio. I think I'm also, like most actors, a child at heart.

I've enjoyed playing both goodies and baddies in my career. I've played some wonderful 'victims' – Claudius (in *I, Claudius*), Alan Turing (*Breaking the Code*), Cyrano De Begerac and Hamlet, and some 'lovely' villains – Richard III, Hitler, etc. The best part about playing 'The Master' was that I was acting in such a legendary series, and I got to act with David Tennant, and also being 'morphed' into John Simm!

Through my career I'm most proud of my work at the Royal Shakespeare Company, the National Theatre and the Prospect Theatre Company, and also *I, Claudius*, *Cadfael* and *Man of Straw*.

When I was a child I was entertained by Hollywood, Westerns and Walt Disney and I was also entertained by pantomimes and comedians like Max Miller and Tommy Trinder, but NEVER clowns!"

A PONTIPINE

DANNY JOHN-JULES
MAID MARION, STORY MAKERS, M.I. HIGH

Danny has appeared in some of the most iconic children's shows of recent years and created some memorable characters along the way. As well as the remake of *The Tomorrow People*, Danny was also the coolest dude in the gang when Maid Marion ruled the roost in Sherwood Forest. Not bad for someone who's famous for evolving from the ship's cat!

"The Cat in *Red Dwarf* has been my most popular role, most of the biggest roles have been on stage, but *Red Dwarf* was collosal and a lot of the kids shows came out of that, and was the reason I got the part in *Maid Marion and her Merry Men*, because someone asked about the guy that was in *Red Dwarf*.

I remember asking Tony what the influences of the show would be, and he said basically, he looked at the shows his kids liked. One was *Blackadder*, for obvious reasons, and the other was *Red Dwarf*. It's got that gawky feel about it. Whacky, surreal and funny as well as being dramatic at times.

The character wasn't called Barrington originally. He was actually called Winston so I had a chat with Tony Robinson and said 'Tony, every black character on television is called Winston, so if you want to come up with something new you really should change the name, or people will just switch off' so they changed his name, but I also had to fight to keep the beard. Because Barrington is a rastafarian, by religion they don't shave, but they said that you can't do comedy with a beard. I begged to differ on that one! Barrington could easily have been a clean shaven Winston!

I did that for 4 years in total. We had an amazing group of supporting artistes who were all in the same theatre group, so they all knew what to do, and interacted so well together and had a lot of fun. Sometimes I watched the background action and it was hysterical.

They say don't work with animals or kids but every job I've done has something to do with both of them. It's a spontaneous thing and that in itself has led me to be in some of the most successful children's shows.

I came from a musical theatre background. Me and Scott Bakula. I was in the musical *Cats* with the choreographer on *Maid Marion*. I did a bit of TV early on and as a dancer I appeared in *The Lena Zavaroni Show* in the 70s – the most famous child performer to come out of this country.

I grew up watching her and reading about her in the newspapers and to think I'd be dancing in her show never even crossed my mind.

I also remember watching the original series of The Tomorrow People and thinking that it was so unusual to see a main character that was black in England.

To have one memorable character in your whole career is very rare. When someone comes up to you from nowhere and says 'It's the Cat!' when you're walking down the road its funny, because people didn't even know my name before then.

I consider Cat and Duane Dibley to be the same person, rather than playing them different characters. I've played many versions of the Cat, and Duane was just one of those versions.

I've been lucky that a lot of my characters have been memorable. Milton Wordsworth from the Story Makers, Lenny Bicknall from M.I. High. I can go all over the world and an english man in a bar will spot me!

Another show I was involved in was Runaway Bay in 1992. I worked with Naomie Harris who I worked with in the Tomorrow People, now she's a big Hollywood star and also with Carl Bradshaw, a famous Jamaican actor who played Ivan in Jimmy Cliff's The Harder They Come.

I've done a lot of voice work too, but people don't really know its me because a lot of the characters have had different types of voices (Barrington was a cockney, Milton was well spoken, and Lenny was an ex-military type) and people have said to me 'I didn't realise you were in Labyrinth, that was one of my favourite films.' I'm a character actor and I like variety. I sung Chilly Down in Labyrinth, and that experience was just something you dream about. First it was a case of getting the job, then it was finding out I'd be recording at Abbey Road Studios with David Bowie, and with Jim Henson watching! It was mad! I've had lots of moments like that. Sword fighting with Wesley Snipes in Blade 2 was another! I've also done a number of audio books and I've worked with Catherine Tate recently on a charity recording.

It's something you dream of sometimes. It's bizarre the people I've run into, some being people I grew up with, particularly in sci-fi circles.

My favourite role though was in a play called *Playboy of the West Indies*, an adaptation of the famous Irish play *Playboy of the Western World*. It was probably my biggest achievement. I had to play the father of a guy on stage who was the same age as me. I had to do my own make up and had to put on a Trinidadian accent. The chips were down! Nick Kent who runs the Shaftesbury Theatre in London was the guy who directed it and gave me the role. It was part of a season of plays. I was also in August Wilson's *The Piano Lesson* playing a preacher.

I got tickets for some people who came to see the show, and some left because they didn't think I was in the play, and didn't know it was me. I sent them a text saying I thought we were going to meet in the bar afterwards. Some had watched the whole play and hadn't realised it was me!

The writer of the play was a guy called Mustapha Matura, who was responsible for the sitcom *No Problem* back in the day, and he said to me 'When Nick told me you had the part I had my reservations, but you are the best young actor I've seen play an old man' and that was worth more to me than anything!"

Danny has a new website
www.dannyjohn-jules.com

RICK JONES
PLAY SCHOOL, FINGERBOBS

"Yoffy lifts a finger, and a mouse appears.." Those were the immortal lines that welcomed me into the world of *Fingerbobs* and had me glued to the box for years. It was unlike anything at the time and it must have struck a creative chord in my pre-school brain. Yoffy's deep, soothing tones and his calm manner were ideal as a storyteller and I think that's why I still remember the programme so fondly to this day. Having bought a DVD of the whole series, it had me mesmerised once again, as it still retained all its charm and humour.

"In 1964, I was appearing with Donald Sutherland, Betsy Blair, Barbara Kelly and Bernard Braden in Edgar Lee Masters' sweet reminiscence of his home town called *Spoon River Anthology*. I won the part in an audition with my ability to read verse, but when it was discovered I sang and played guitar, the musical duties, (American Folk Songs of that period) fell mainly to me and a lovely lady called Isla Cameron. I was miffed at the time, as I so loved to display my acting talents with really good material like this – I suggest you obtain a copy and read it; it's a wonderful posthumous exposé of the denizens of a small community as illustrated by the discrepancies between their epitaphs written on stone, and the truth of their lives in town – but as the production wore on I realised it was an equal honour to sing the great folk tunes to full houses every night, and, of course, in light of ensuing events, it was seminal. Joy Whitby, a children's producer at the BBC attended the show one evening and came backstage to invite me to join the production team of a new children's show called *Play School*.

I was married with two children, and although 'kiddies entertainment' had never crossed my mind as a career path, needs must when the Devil drives. I accepted, and with it came a modicum of financial stability, since, although the BBC was ALWAYS a notoriously stingy payer, the shows were repeated daily, which doubled the money and made it attractive. My wife at the time, I remember, was pleased.

Julie Stevens, who became a lifelong friend, I believe was the first girl I worked the show with, but it may have been Virginia Stride, or even Carol Chell – after all these years and SO MANY round or square windows, it's all a bit misty...

I believe 'Yoffy' is Hebrew for 'Happy', or 'Cheerful' or somesuch. It was the work of Joanne and Michael Cole, two of the sweetest humans who ever graced this planet. They are no longer with us, worse luck, but if they were I'd go anywhere and do anything for them – they were the creative engine and allowed me carte blanche for all the silliness that occurred. It was such hard work scooting around under tables with one's fingers up little animals' bums, that we finally engineered a system of slings on runners so I could whizz about manically down there

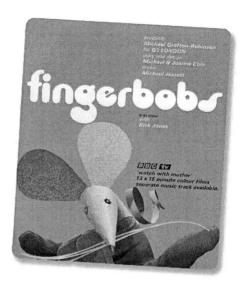

trying desperately to remember which character to stick up which entrance on what cue. I lost weight. Some of the fairy dust got scraped off when I discovered that I'd been tricked into signing a contract with an outside contractor who had not promised to pay residuals, so none of the many years of repeat after repeat netted me one penny. I felt betrayed, as I'd given them everything I could. It was the deceit of the Producer, (whose name has happily faded from memory) that caused this miscarriage, but as I was soon in Hollywood producing a musical I'd written with two friends, even his pasty face has dissolved into the waters of forgetfulness. The show brought children to me everywhere I went, and their is no finer approbation than the glee of children. *Fingerbobs* himself, or, I suppose I should say 'itself', remains though as a constant reminder of the little studio in Covent Garden, and the wonderful cameraman who'd covered every war up until then and had had enough war John Abbot – he conspired with me on the last day of shooting to NOT cut the camera on command, but leave it running as I sneaked the struggling Fingermouse into the dregs of my coffee cup and drowned the little beggar! What joy. That's a wrap!

Before Children's TV I had played Mercutio to Jane Asher's Juliet – I believe David Weston played Romeo – for Rediffusion, to further nail the period - I'd been a long-serving member of David Scase's Manchester Library Theatre, with Anthony Hopkins, Garfield Morgan et al, in what was considered it's heyday, where I originated a role in a play called *You've Never Had It So Good*, which also played at Coventry Rep with Trevor Nunn, the lovely man directing, and did *Orlando*, Antony, the lead in *Five Finger Exercise* –

(Scase said my accent was more Arab than German, but the performance just managed to save me. David Scase was one of the great rough diamonds of the British Theatre at that time – extremely leftish, perhaps a Communist, who always found the hidden social comment in Shakespeare and made it funny. I miss him, and he should be written about. I toured the States with a company called Theatre Outlook. We played the big Uni's and when we got to St. Loius the manager got caught by creditors and duffed up in an alley, leaving him and us without funds. U.S. Equity found us fares home, and we played our hotel bill at the Sheraton by performing a Restoration comedy for nothing. Ah Art!!

I stayed alive previous to *Play School* by doing voice work under the tutelage of Louis Elman at De Lane Lea studios – another knight undubbed, as it were – we did *Belle and Sebastien*, and a kid's TV thing about French Aeronauts, and THAT netted me my first theme song – Higher than high boys, we're up in the sky boys da dum did de dum dum the Daredevil Aeronauts etc. Odd what you'll do to earn a loaf.

After an overzealous fan sent me two huge joints, addressing them to the 'Head of Children's TV', which obviously hastened my metamorphosis from 'actor' to 'musician', I concentrated on songwriting and music for a few years, working with Len Black at Active Music in Tin Pan Alley (actually 142 Charing Cross Road) where we wrote for Georgie Fame and Kiki Dee and oh, you get the picture. I sang in The Pickwick Club – partly owned by the father of my friend Gered Mankowitz, the renowned rock photog, where (although this was only one of dozens of amazing things that happened to me in this club) I sang a particular song to the Beatles – they were all sitting in one booth, and listened gracefully. I still blush considering my song choice.

Terry Stamp and I had gone to drama school together (Webber-Douglas) and we bumped into each other from time to time after we were working actors. He told me, in a pub behind Charing Cross, about this terrific group called *The Silver Beatles*, he'd seen in Liverpool – probably when he was touring in *Taste of Honey*. 'They're going to be enormous! Bigger than Sinatra!', is how he put it. So when the Maitre'D at the Pickwick whispered in my ear 'Look – it's the Silver

Beatles' I knew who was walking into the club, having been clued by the prescient Terrence Stamp. I waited until they had found a booth, then sauntered over and strummed out my rather sweet version of *I Gave My Love A Cherry* – a soppy old folk song more suited to Andy Williams than the Fab Four. But of course, they *weren't* the Fab Four then – they were just four nice kids from Liverpool, only too happy to be boozing in a nice London club mid-afternoon, and even tolerant to the resident folk singer. I mean, I knew lots of Bill Broonsy, Josh White, roots blues, you name it, but for some unknown reason chose to sing that old folk tune. They were charming, John grabbed my old Levin nylon string and flew about on it a bit, and they bought me a Canadian Club and ginger ale – my tipple at the time. Ah – take me back! Let me sing 'em *Maggie's Farm* or something. Please!

No one ever gave me any advice about anything regarding children's TV. Just as well really, I wasn't the type to listen to it. Still the same, I suppose – at least I listen now – I have no regrets regarding my associations with the BBC TV and Children's Entertainment in general. It led me into the music business, which toughened me and prepared me for my years in a Rock and Roll band called *Meal Ticket* with Willy Finlayson, Steve Simpson, Chris Hunt, and Ray Flacke - all more talented musically than me, but in need of an idiot to write songs for them which, with the help of the amazing Dave Pierce,

I did, all the while, with Pierce and another Canadian called Steve Hammond, (a man who could listen to Sibelius and jot down the score as if he were taking shorthand) we wrote *Flash Fearless vs The Zzorgwomen chapters 5&6* which eventually went on stage in Hollywood in 1981, and that event set me on my present course. I pray for a steady wind. The sea sounds like the laughter of children."

You can purchase Rick's latest album "Life Drawing" at CD Baby or on iTunes. www.ricknval.com

RICK JONES

SHARI LEWIS & LAMB CHOP
THE SHARI LEWIS SHOW

Shari Lewis was a ground breaking and multi-award winning ventriloquist and puppeteer, and after her passing, her daughter Mallory, herself an award winning writer and performer, made sure that Lamb Chop could be loved by future generations by continuing to perform with the loveable sheep throughout America. I spoke with Mallory, ironically, on the 11th anniversary of her mother's passing.

"My grandfather was known as Peter Pan the Magic Man in New York who did juggling, magic, balloons and puppetry, and my mom had a puppet called Taffy Twinkle, a silly farmgirl, who was a standard ventriloquist type dummy, but that puppet was hated, and so mom made another and created Lamb Chop to take over from Taffy.

Mom very quickly got on the *Captain Kangaroo* TV show with her act and that's when her career took off.

I loved it when my mom came to Britain to do the *Shari Lewis Show* in the 70s. She also did 3 Royal Command performances. I was about 8 at the time and mom put me into camp, and it was great — riding horses through the streets. That would never happen in America. Johnny Downes was the producer of the show, and he was shocked that one of Shari's daughters was a hippy! I later worked with mom as a producer and head writer on her shows.

KERMIT & LAMB CHOP

Shari loved being an entertainer, all of whom have a need for clapping, and she loved the skill and discipline of puppetry.

I took over performing with Lamb Chop about 10 years ago. I was accepting a lot of posthumous awards after her passing, and it's not something I could make a living doing! So, I decided to give it a shot myself, and Lamb Chop returned. I dyed my hair red and changed my surname to Lewis in her honour just make it easier — something my husband suggested. Some people say 'You look like your mom', well I do have some genetic links too!

SHARI & MALLORY – 1992/93 DAY TIME EMMY AWARDS – OUTSTANDING WRITING IN A CHILDREN'S SERIES.
FIRST EMMY EVER TO BE WON SIMULTANEOUSLY BY A MOTHER AND DAUGHTER.

Shari was on TV every day in the 90s in America with *Lamb Chop's Play-Along* which is still being shown, so another generation can grow up with Lamb Chop.

I love interacting with the audience. Lamb Chop brings such a look of joy to people and it's lovely to see people's inner 3 year old!

We've appeared on USO performing to the troops and recently we've performed a series of shows at the Ohio State Festival. My 10 year old son has been adopted by a troupe of jugglers! He learns so quickly. He travels with me and helps backstage and hooks up my sound – the 4th generation in the entertainment industry!

My mom loved working in the UK and Lamb Chop would love to be on British TV once again!"

You can keep up to date with Lamb Chop at www.lambchop.tv

LAMB CHOP & MALLORY

PETER LLEWELLYN-JONES
MR. GRIMLEY – THE RIDDLERS

For 10 years The Riddlers – messrs Mossop and Tiddler and Middler – solved problems from their base in a well in the magical garden of Marjorie Dawe, with each episode revolving around a fable from the Riddlestone. Mr. Grimley, the chimney sweep, was also doing his own kind of teaching off screen with a successful career in teaching and sign language. A lesson for us all!

"I'd done a drama course after I left school, but I soon got into working with deaf children as a social worker, and my involvement with deaf children grew from there. I also worked on HTV interpreting the news.

In 1980 I got a job on a big crime serial set in London called *Fox* with Peter Vaughn, Liz Spriggs, Ray Winstone and Larry Lamb. They wanted a deaf child, and I became the programme consultant. They also gave me a bit-part in the serial as a teacher.

I also did some writing and wrote scripts for a show called *Insight* for Yorkshire Television with Victoria Wood.

It was common in those days for researchers to be able to progress to be producers, so things gradually developed.

There was a programme called *Our World* which was a weekly Junior School's programme which ran for 7 years and the team behind that were also working on *The Riddlers* at the same time. I knew all the backroom team and they needed someone to play Mr. Grimley. There wasn't really any casting, you'd be given parts, and it was a case of being in the right place at the right time, and it worked out well for me.

You have to suspend disbelief when working with puppets, especially when there is a big bearded bloke underneath laying on a trolley. Even at roadshows kids would talk to the puppet even though the guys operating them were in full view.

Whilst being in The Riddlers I was also teaching at University in term times with the filming done in one block during the summer break.

We were like one big family based at YTV (who made a lot of schools' programmes) and I got to know Neil Innes and I got to work on *The Riddlers* theme music.

After *The Riddlers* I did the odd thing here and there - corporate presenting and guest appearances on TV and radio. Acting wasn't my career. It was great fun to do but I had another job I could do and I'd already started writing post-graduate courses for university. You get too old for kids TV in the end. Kids don't relate to fat old men!

My new students tend to laugh when they realise I was in *The Riddlers* and some are gobsmacked. It usually takes 2-3 weeks before they start asking questions about it. They would tell me that they used to watch me when they were 4 or 5 years old, and I would say 'It's not done my academic career any harm!'

Teaching is what I do. I've done it for 30 years and I really enjoy it and ultimately it gives me the most satisfaction. I wouldn't have missed the chance of working on TV. There wasn't any conflict and I got the best of both worlds.

During the summer months I got to dress as a twit and fall in a pool – it was a very balancing thing to do."

WILF LUNN
VISION ON, JIGSAW, EUREKA, MAGPIE

Wilf Lunn, fellow Yorkshireman and inventor extraordinaire, was prominent in the 60s, 70s and 80s on a variety of shows. Famed for his coloured spectacles and facial topiary, Wilf also has the honour of being the sixth Doctor before Colin Baker!

"I first started writing and making miniature bicycles (out of firewood wire) when I was teaching lip-reading & religious knowledge at *Odsal House School For the Deaf* in Yorkshire.

The parents of the film star James Mason lived on the same street as us, in Huddersfield, and I met James when he was visiting them. He advised me only to write about subjects within my experience. I had already written a TV play called *Benny Rolly* which, unusually for the time, was without dialogue.

James introduced me to an agent, Blanche Marvin. She thought that, since my play had no dialogue, it would be of interest to the deaf so she arranged an interview with Patrick Dowling the producer of *Vision On* and I took along some of my models. He said he couldn't use me, but suggested I should have an exhibition of my cycles, which Blanche arranged. On the opening night, Joan Bakewell, the TV presenter, visited and asked me if I'd like to be on television. Being slightly the worse for drink I said, 'Yes ...when?' to which she replied, 'Tonight!' and so, I did my first TV show, *Late Night Line Up*.

After that I was invited to appear on *Magpie*, a rival children's show to *Blue Peter*, with Sue Stranks and a Canadian water skier. I was

WILF'S APOCALYPSE COW

asked if I could do something other than talk about cycles, so I did one show about bottles and one about the history of the domestic smoothing iron.

In the meantime Patrick Dowling approached me about making a 'door bell machine'. I had never done anything like that before but I said 'Yes'.

I appeared with the machine on *Vision On*, the award-winning programme which I appeared on for many years alongside Tony Hart. He was the main guy and a really nice guy.

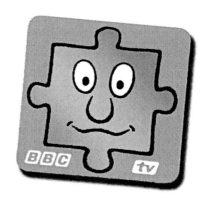

I went onto *Jigsaw* with Sylvester McCoy, Janet Ellis and David Rappaport and then *Eureka* and *Fun Factory*, both with Jeremy Beadle.

In 1979 Jeremy Beadle did a late night programme for L.B.C. (London Broadcasting Company). One day he bought a toy ray gun from Hamley's. When the trigger was pulled it made a strange sound, which he used during his show pretending he was talking to a space robot called Kurt Knobbler. Despite the sounds being meaningless, people would phone the show to talk to the robot and Kurt even got fan mail.

When L.B.C. got a stand at the Ideal Home Exhibition, they realised that lots of people would be coming to see Kurt who, of course, only existed as a sound effect. Jeremy asked me to build a robot. KURT was a great success and went on to appear on the children's TV show *Jigsaw* and a series *Fun Factory* for Granada TV. Despite the fact that Kurt was no longer on *Jigsaw*, the show still gave him a mention in the credits – 'Kurt Knobbler did not appear'

From *Fun Factory*, Kurt did pantomime in Liverpool and was last seen holding a fork full of peas in a Newbury restaurant.

I'd previously worked with Sylvester McCoy on *Vision On*, and he later went on to play *Doctor Who*, I played the Doctor for a sketch on *Jigsaw* – it was a version of the famous Abbott & Costello sketch 'Who's on first', so I actually got to play the Doctor before he did, and before Colin Baker, so I was the REAL sixth Doctor Who!

KURT KNOBBLER

Talking of *Doctor Who*, the actor Ken Campbell got an american kid to ring up the Beeb to ask if there was any truth in the rumour that Ken was to be the next Doctor, rather than audition! He was a crafty bugger.

There's an outtake on YouTube of me swearing on a programme called *What's the Idea?* I was stood on a golf course in Liverpool demonstrating my 'Owl Scarer' device, which consisted of fireworks attached to a helmet that was strapped to my head. The crew fixed the camera then ran off and left me to it!

I found that in my life, I set out to do something and put a lot of effort in to it but when I show the project to someone they say 'That's very nice but could you do this for us instead'. For example, when I got some publicity for putting a bicycle in a bottle, the only interest that was shown was by a man who telephoned me to ask, 'Are you the man that put a bicycle in a bottle?' When I excitedly replied that I was, he said, 'You can help me… I reckon that if you can put a bicycle in a bottle you'll be able to show me how to make a three-piece suite cheaper than any one else.'

Now I write an article for my local newspaper, the Huddersfield Examiner. I don't think my work is suitable for kids TV these days as it involves a lot of explosions, but who knows."

You can read more about Wilf's creations and purchase his autobiography to the age of 11 'My Best Cellar' at www.wilflunn.com

LIZZIE McPHEE
WIZADORA

Wizadora was the tales of a trainee wizard, in a time when Harry Potter was just a twinkle in his dad's wand! Lizzie was the second incarnation, and the show followed her day to day dealings with Tatty Bogle, Stan the Shopkeeper, a barking doormat, a talking coat hangar, a squeaking vegetable and three people who lived in a chest of drawers. Respect! *Wizadora*, we adore her!

"How I got to be *Wizadora* was quite a bizarre series of events. I was a serious theatre actor at the time, involved with the Political Theatre Company at the Red Room and wanting to change the world. I was in a play called *Sunspots* by Judy Upton and the other girl in the play kept going to auditions for a kids TV programme. They had been looking for someone for ages and she kept being re-called. One day she came back really upset because she didn't get the part.

Then my agent put me forward for an audition for *Wizadora*, and it just happened to be the same part this girl had been going for! I went along and had a screen test, and the execs came to see me in the play which was pretty hardcore stuff - having sex on stage every night - but the execs must have liked what they saw because I got the job!

They received 1500 submissions from agents, but because I went along thinking that this would just be a nice job, and wasn't desperate for a career in children's TV, coupled with the travelling I'd done, they said they found me interesting, and I think that helped me get the part.

I was on the show for 3 years in total and maybe I didn't really appreciate how much I enjoyed it at the time as I was a quite intense actor, but looking back on it now it was a great time and definitely the most fun in my career. People in kids TV come across as being very clean cut, but there was a lot of innuendo and naughtiness on set, which made it so much fun!

I was popular among students who said I was a more wild, naughty and spunky Wizadora. I think the dads liked me as well whereas the mums liked the previous Wizadora as she was sweeter than me. At the time I was quite shy to do publicity for the show. I was on *This is Your Life*, and other kids TV programmes as Wizadora but I also saw myself as a serious political actor as well, but *Wizadora* helped me to see the world. I did panto every year as Wizadora and it was very well paid and I used the money from that to go travelling annually.

The filming of the show was pretty full on. We filmed 36 episodes at a time, but it was such fun nevertheless. The director was Alistair Clarke who was really nice and was very good to me and had welcomed me with open arms. *Wizadora* was his baby, he loved the show and all the team. The following series though, they announced we were to have a change of director which was devastating to Alistair, and at first we were worried it wouldn't have the same feel to it, and a few of us were thinking 'Should we do the next series?' in support of Alistair, but in this line of work you're always replaceable, and you have to keep paying your rent, and because I loved playing Wizadora as well, we decided to carry on – we were like a family after all. As it turned out, the new Executive Producer was very good creatively and we did some good work despite the changes. Brian Murphy (who played Stan the Shopkeeper) is the most fantastic guy I've ever worked with. A very humble guy and a comic genius!

Wizadora ended when a new controller came in at CITV and basically wanted some new programmes, so that was that.

After *Wizadora* I carried on acting in plays and on TV. I'm most proud of my theatre work, but I've also had a lot of variety in my career, playing a drug addict one moment, then *Wizadora* the next!

I've appeared in a one-woman show, wrote a play about suicide and I also played a teacher in a Ruth Rendell story – all the kids on set were going crazy with excitement because their teacher was Wizadora!

I have my own children now and it's such a life changing event. The previous Wizadora stopped, I believe, because she had children, and I can understand why. I've been keeping my hand in but maybe once my children go to school I'll get more involved in acting once again.

If *Wizadora* came back I'd probably be a little too old now to play her again, but I wouldn't want anyone else to play her either" ☺

LIZZIE McPHEE

NICK MERCER
PLAY SCHOOL, GREENCLAWS, STORY MAKERS

Prolific and versatile are two words that could easily describe Nick Mercer. Whether its on-screen, in a costume or under a desk, Nick has had a long career in children's televisual entertainment, but a face that you might not immediately recognise. Nick is renowned for his amazing array of character voices, something that has stood him in good stead during his career.

"I was a presenter on the final series of *Play School* in 1987/8, and the then series producer (Christine Hewitt) then went on to devise a new series which turned out to be *Greenclaws*; Believing me to be easy-going and physically up to it, she asked me if I'd like to play the big green monster. She also thought I had a good range of character voices which would be useful for all the stories 'Claws was going to tell about his famous relatives.

It was a very strange and new experience to be working inside a 'Skin' – obviously very hot and sweaty, and a good deal of sensory deprivation: I was cut off from the studio by a thick layer of foam rubber and latex so it was difficult to hear and see what was going on around me. The eye holes were tiny, which meant I had very limited tunnel vision; I could also glance down out of his nostrils for anything that had to be seen lower than his eye-line. This actually made it look as if he really was searching for stuff in his short-sighted way.

My voice was done 'live' from inside the Skin – rather than being pre or post-recorded – which was good as it meant that I could play and react spontaneously everything that went on – the downside being that all that talking made it a lot more sweaty and stuffy in the suit (I did a few skin-jobs after *Greenclaws*, where the voice was pre-recorded – and it does make a massive difference). Actually, I think the slightly breathless quality added to Greenclaws' voice and personality.

I'm not sure what Health & Safety would make of it these days! The head itself took a couple of minutes to get on and off. We used to aim for 20 to 30 minutes in the skin, and then I'd come up for air and barley water. When we had standing-round moments the dresser would blow one of those battery operated fans through Greenclaws' mouth to get a bit of air circulating! It was quite an experience getting back into the skin after lunch – rather like climbing into a giant, clammy wet sponge....

There were two dressers (Tracey in series 1 and Giles in series 2) who did far more than their job would normally require. They would be holding the mouth of the costume open, mopping my sweaty brow and towelling my head (we found a Number one head -shave to be most comfortable for the two months duration of filming), putting in a hand fan, supplying fluids etc Often I'd get them to quickly run the lines with me, or hold the script up to the eye-holes so I could check stuff before recording.

After the show finished, the suit went into storage, and was then offered to me for a 'token fee'. I think I paid about £100 for a costume that cost about £6,000 to make! My sister kept it in her garden shed for a while (which was kind of fitting) but the mice took a fancy to it. I still have the head, claws, feet, tail and waistcoat and spectacles but all looking a bit faded now.

I didn't really talk much about Greenclaws when I did it – the target audience could only be disappointed by having some mouthy actor saying 'Yeah – that's me in that green rubber suit!' – but in the last few years people have started asking me about it (it appears on my biography in theatre programmes etc), saying they remembered the programme.
In my experience, some people never saw it, but the people that did see it REALLY liked it – and there are some lovely comments on YouTube and other websites.

After Greenclaws I did more 'conventional' acting work – theatre and radio and a few bits and pieces on TV – and then I did three years on Playdays after Clare Bradley (who I had met as an assistant floor manager on Play School, and was now a Producer for Felgates TV) called me in for an interview. She had remembered me mentioning that I played a couple of instruments, and they were casting a character called Charlie Grindle, a kind of musical Mr. Fix-it.

Part of the Playdays job was also to puppeteer and voice a character called Morris, and I decided that the puppeteering for television was something I really enjoyed – and so I started to go for more of those jobs. Some people train in puppetry (and indeed actually make and maintain the puppets they work with) and some people just fall into it – I'm in the latter category obviously, but after I'd got a few series under my belt, I began to feel less like an interloper! And, again, the character voices that I do were useful for this kind of work.

Clare Bradley came up with a new series in 2000 – Story Makers – set in a magical children's library after midnight. I puppeteered and voiced Jackson – a pink furry character who, with his frog-like friend Jelly, would help create the stories in each programme. We ended up doing four series and 250 programmes in total. Jelly and Jackson also worked as presenters on the Cbeebies' versions of *Springwatch* and *Autumnwatch* and were guests on a *Weakest Link* puppet special, getting to Round 6 before being voted off by Roland Rat and Sue from *The Sooty Show*!

I do a fair bit of cartoon work. On *Story Makers* I had a whole cartoon to myself – voicing all the characters in *Blue Cow*, and I've also worked on *Those Scurvy Rascals, Tommy Zoom, Wonder Pets* and *3rd and Bird*.

For the last four years I've played Timon, the Meerkat in Disney's production of *The Lion King*, at the Lyceum Theatre in London. Timon is portrayed by a fantastic and beautiful Bunraku puppet, almost as big as me. I'm not hidden but I'm connected to every part so it moves with me – I manipulate the head and left arm, but it seems that every part of him is alive! And guess what…? I'm green from head to toe! – wig, make-up, costume, the lot! so that really does seem to be my colour!

I seem to have spent a good deal of the last 20 odd years working hidden inside skins, under puppets or voicing characters – It's fantastically satisfying work and you get used to being contorted into different shapes, hiding under tables etc, and also coming up with ever more idiosyncratic voices... certainly an unusual job!"

To see Nick in action in *The Lion King* visit www.lyceum-theatre.co.uk

NICK MERCER

LIONEL MORTON
PLAY SCHOOL, PLAYAWAY

It really doesn't matter if it's raining or it's fine, just as long as you've got time to read the memories of Lionel Morton. Play Schooler, *Playaway* signature tune writer and former chart topper. Lionel's musical background has stood him in good stead, and this Blackburn born singer/songwriter's career has seen him take on a host of top West End roles as well as being best friends with Humpty and the gang.

"I've always been a singer. I started when I was 8 years old, and I was a soprano cathedral chorister until I was 15, travelling Britain singing in such illustrious venues as the Royal Albert Hall and St. Paul's Cathedral, as well as recording and broadcasting for the BBC.

The very first record I bought was *Rock Around the Clock* and it inspired me to play the guitar. I taught myself to play and for a few years toured the working men's club circuit. In 1962 I formed *The Lionel Morton Four*, which then became *The Four Pennies*. It was a great time to be part of the pop scene during the Swinging 60s! In 1964 we wrote a song called *Juliet* which reached No. 1 in the charts. There were a lot of one-hit wonders around at that time, but we did have another song *Black Girl* which also charted.

We were together for about 5 years until the bubble had burst. We could have gone on to do Christmas pantos or do a summer season, and we had an offer to be a resident act on the northern cabaret circuit, but I didn't fancy doing that again, so I wound it up myself.

Looking back, we did have a song under our belt *Until its Time For You to Go* and if we'd released that as our second single, I think it would have gone to No. 1 as well. Elvis went on to have a hit with it in the 70s!

I went on to join *Play School*, where I met Rick Jones. It was a wonderful time, and the people were so nice to work with. The BBC had a children's TV department and an adult entertainment department, but *Play School* wasn't in either category because it was aimed at under fives, so we were basically left alone in the East Tower

PLAYING TONY IN WEST SIDE STORY

of Television Centre to do our own thing. We were given free reign and the approach by the crew and presenters to the production was good.

I was advised to think of there being just one child sitting at home. (It was shown at about 11am then), so when I looked into the lens I would think of that one child so it made it feel more personal. I'd say something like 'We can do this...' but I would add 'if you want' so it gave the child an in or out option, in case they weren't able to. I was also the first presenter to have an accent. Up until then it had all been very proper BBC English.

While on *Play School* I was approached to write a theme tune for a new show *Playaway*. It was a bit of a tongue twister with its P.L.A.Y playaway-way-playaway-a-play, playaway-way-a-playaway-playaway.

It used a 'donkey jaw' instrument — actually made from the jaw of a donkey — to create that distinctive rattle on every 4th beat, and they loved it.

I was asked to present the programme and so myself, Brian Cant, Toni Arthur

LIONEL IN JESUS CHRIST SUPERSTAR

and the musician Jonathan Cohen were initially the four main presenters, with others such as Johnny Ball guesting on some shows. I don't think any of them, apart from Jonathan, could get their mouths round the lyrics. I'm sure you can see them struggling on the videos!

I can't go anywhere without people asking me to do the *Playaway* theme. I worked with a guy recently who, when he found out I'd written that song, he got so excited and was saying 'you're a legend.' It's nice to be immortalised on celluloid.

After 3-4 years on the show I found out it was going to transfer into the theatres, and I didn't particularly want to do that, so I knocked it on the head. 4 years doing one thing is enough, I think. Children's entertainment is fine, so long as it doesn't take over things. Brian Cant was a brilliant actor and I think, despite him being so brilliant and well loved as a children's presenter, he would have liked to have done more serious acting than he did.

I actually presented *Playaway* and *Play School* whilst I was appearing in shows in the West End. I sang the role of Jesus in *Jesus Christ Superstar*, and I also played Tony in *West Side Story*. I'd often ask for a couple of days off from my theatre workload so I could fit in my TV work. It was a busy time. One day I'd be playing Jesus Christ, the next day I'd be looking through the square window!

THE FOUR PENNIES

One of my claims to fame is that I was the very first 'Owl' in David Wood's musical adaptation of Edward Leer's *The Owl and the Pussycat went to Sea* which we performed at the Jeannetta Cochrane Theatre and it went on to run in the West End at Christmas for many years. We would do 3 shows in a day, at 3pm, 5pm and 7.30pm. I've also played the lead, Claude, in the rock musical *Hair*.

I think the musicals were probably the apex of my career. I have to say it was powerful stuff to be playing Jesus Christ on a Good Friday and at Christmas and seeing rows of nuns all sobbing into their habits!

I'm now living happily in Cornwall with my partner of 25 years and with my 4 lovely children."

LIONEL MORTON

SUE NICHOLLS
PIPKINS, RENTAGHOST

Confession time. Nadia Popov was one of my first childhood crushes and definitely one of my favourite characters. Maybe it was that accent, the ribbons in her hair or the cute sneeze that did it! Now a star of *Coronation Street*, Sue has had a varied career, working with ghosts and ghouls and freaks and fools, and a scraggy old hare that would have got Fred Elliott's back up. Pray silence please for the Honourable (and charming) Susan Nicholls.

"*Pipkins* was a wonderful time. I was in the last 2 or 3 series playing the next door neighbour, Mrs Muddle. It was great fun. I'd done a little bit of kids TV before that, but I soon realised you can have much more fun and giggles!

I loved working with Hartley Hare. He was so funny and sweet, I always wanted to take him home with me! Nigel Plaskitt voiced and operated Hartley and he went on to work on *Spitting Image*, and more recently he's the man behind the PG Tips Monkey, and also my closest friend.

Being from the West Midlands, the great thing about playing Mrs Muddle was being able to use my own accent, and one of my claims to fame (in the days when filming didn't stop) was Mrs Muddle having to actually make an omelette live on screen. I was very starry eyed wondering if I could make it, with no TV chef to help me, but I did!

In the early 1960s I was, thankfully, a working actress, working in the theatre all over the country, then life took off for me in 1964 when I was in the original soap opera *Crossroads* playing Marilyn Gates. Thankfully, the character took off and I stayed with the show until 1969.

I also had a successful pop record and did some cabaret and singing, and other TV work of the day included *Duchess of Duke Street* and *Dixon of Dock Green*. I even worked with the lovely Pauline Quirke when she was just a child in ATV's *Children's Ward*.

Originally I wanted to do musicals as I love to sing and dance, and enjoy the lighter side of life. I'm not into Shakespeare and Checkov even though that's what you start out with as a student at R.A.D.A!

Rentaghost was enormous fun. Linda La Plante was originally playing a ghosty nurse. She was a fabulous actress and comedian but at the time she was also writing *Widows*. She eventually left the show because she wanted to concentrate on her writing, therefore leaving a gap in the ghost market.

Jeremy Swan, who is a huge friend now, was producer/director of *Rentaghost* and they wanted someone Eastern European, so Nadia Popov was born. It was enormous fun with lots of giggles. When I walked down the street builders would sneeze at me!

I also worked alongside Christopher Biggins and we'd be misbehaving in front of the camera and not realising, and Jeremy would tell us off in no uncertain terms. I'd like to thank Lynda for leaving, and giving me such a fun opportunity.

Michael Staniforth, who played Timothy Claypole, was a lovely man, who was totally mad on screen and even madder off. So energetic and bouncy, in fact all of the cast were lovely. Ann Emery, who played Mrs Meaker, was madder than any of us! She's one of the best tap dancers around, even better than Michael, and she is now brilliantly playing Billy Elliot's grandmother in the West End.

Rentaghost certainly appealed to the kids although I don't think my mum necessarily understood what it was about. It had some wonderful gags written by Bob Block, and despite our childishness it was very much part of my life. I still have my *Rentaghost* t-shirt, and sometimes tease them at the Corrie studio by saying 'I think I'll put Nadia's ribbons in Audrey's hair today for a change!'

I was told never work with kids and animals, but I've loved working with children and, albeit, puppet animals. The children I've worked with have been totally lovely, despite some who might have a diva moment, but it's usually the adults who have been responsible for the diva moments rather than the little ones!

I remember being a guest on a game show *The Adventure Game* in 1980 with the swimmer Duncan Goodhew. We had to work out how to get round this assault course, jumping through hoops and the like, but we managed to get there in the end.

I've been in *Coronation Street* since 1979 and joined permanently in 1984 having started my working life in the theatre in 1960 and I've not regretted it a bit.

HARTLEY AND MRS MUDDLE

Actually, now, my time on the 'Street' has been longer than the rest of my career put together. It's been lovely to have done a bit of everything, mainly because, in the early days, I took most of the jobs I was offered as I wanted to gain the experience.

As a kid I used to watch Annette Mills and *Muffin the Mule*, but life wasn't so telly orientated in the 40s and 50s, and cinema wasn't really on the agenda. Now one of my favourite children's programmes is *Angelina Ballerina*. I bought the DVD of the series and reverted back to childhood! Judy Dench did the voice over and I like to think her accent was similar to a huskier Nadia Popov! I can imagine kids watching that sitting cross-legged just like me as a grown up!

Being in the 'Street' is wonderful but it does eat up your life. My husband lives in London and I live in Manchester and my filiming schedule is always so full on and tight that we can't plan anything ahead, even holidays have to be booked 4 or 5 months in advance for the sake of the writers.

Audrey has her ups and downs and you're never quite sure what will happen next, but I was terribly flattered to win 'Best Comedy Performance' at the 2000 British Soap Awards and the 'Hero of the Year' and 'Best Dramatic Performance' awards for the Richard Hillman storyline in 2003. Saying that, they're still in their boxes in my dressing room as I just haven't got anywhere to put them.

Awards are very flattering, and I'd be silly to say I'm not chuffed to get them, but I hope youngsters don't go into the industry just for the awards. They should always try and do the best they can. Awards are just a nice bonus, and also very heavy!"

SUE NICHOLLS

ROY NORTH
MR. ROY – BASIL BRUSH, GET IT TOGETHER

When I received a phone call one day, and the man on the end of the line said "Hello, it's Mr. Roy" a large smile grew across my face, followed by a series of pleasant flashbacks! This Hull City supporting actor and presenter was, for four years, the faithful companion of everyone's favourite bushy-tailed, boom-booming fox.

"I'd been out of drama school for seven years, merrily doing theatre work, until one day, the actor Melvin Hayes told me about an audition after helping him move his fridge. Basil Brush was looking for a new friend.

I was one of 50 people who auditioned, and I got the job. It was very nerve wracking at first, having never done any TV work before in front of a live audience. I was introduced to the audience and it freaked me out at first, but I learnt to be myself.

Basil had started in the mid 1960's, a creation of Ivan Owen and George Martin, who was a terrific script writer. Ivan always kept away from the limelight, but he created magic - like Santa - and the show attracted a host of famous guests, such as David Nixon.

They wrote their own series with Derek Fowlds working alongside Basil for 4 series, then I took over and did another 4 series, and the show became part of Saturday evening's TV line up alongside *Doctor Who, Starsky and Hutch* and *The Generation Game* - straight after *Grandstand*.

Working with Basil was like being part of a double act and it was a real 1-to-1 relationship. In 1976 we were invited to Jim Callaghan's Christmas party at No. 10. It was for underprivileged kids, and it was a terrific experience all round. No. 10 is like a TARDIS inside. George used to stick in the odd innuendo into the script, and it really made the kids and dads laugh.

I ended up appearing in pantos with Basil and we even did a 10 week tour of New Zealand.

I went on to present *Get it Together* - a kids pop show for Granada. I did nearly 100 programmes and it got around 4 million viewers on Thursday afternoons. I would have liked to have done both programmes but it wasn't possible to do them simultaneously.

GET IT TOGETHER 1979

I found it quite tricky to make the transition from kids presenting to adults, so I decided to go back to acting. I've been a member of Northern Broadsides since 1992. They're a theatre company who put on Shakespeare's plays with northern accents. I'm from Hull originally but learnt to lose my accent for my TV work. I've also done some work with the Hull Truck Theatre Company.

These days I'm spending my pension on football. I've been a follower of Hull City since 1952 and I'm a season ticket holder. I used to play showbiz football back in the 70's alongside Rod Stewart, Robert Lindsay, Dave Dee and Ed Stewart. I'm a natural left footer and played wide on the left, and played at Fulham, Chelsea and Wembley. Ron Atkinson was our manager and treated us just like he would with professionals."

PETER PURVES
DOCTOR WHO, BLUE PETER

Peter holds the unique distinction of being involved in two of the longest running children's shows on British TV! Having travelled in the TARDIS Peter joined the *Blue Peter* team as a stop gap and ended up staying for over 10 years, becoming part of what is now known as the 'Dream Team' with Valerie Singleton and John Noakes, whilst also taking charge of the beloved *Blue Peter* dog Petra.

"Following a couple of leading roles in TV plays I heard that *Doctor Who* was looking for actors who could 'move' to play giant butterflies and other insects in one of the serials. I went along to meet the director, Richard Martin, who very kindly told me that with the work I had been doing previously it wasn't worth me playing one of the non-speaking roles. However, he told me that if ever he was casting proper acting parts, he would think of me.

A few months later Richard was true to his word when he cast me as Morton Dill in *The Chase*. I was thrilled to be playing the part, but even more thrilled when I was asked to go with the Producer, Verity Lambert, for a drink at Studio 3, the pub opposite the Riverside Studios. I was dumbfounded when she asked me if I would be interested in joining the cast on a regular basis. Naturally I said 'Yes' and Steven Taylor made his debut appearance three weeks later opposite the first Doctor, William Hartnell.

Of all the serials the historical ones were my favourites - particularly *The Massacre* and *The Myth Makers* – and I have quite an affection for *The Celestial Toymaker*.

I finally left the cast of the show in June 1966.

More recently it has been a delight to be involved again. The remastered CDs being launched required some new commentary to add continuity to the original sound tracks and it has been a privilege to have narrated all of the stories in which I took part.

Blue Peter was a brilliant mixture of fun and hard work – I honestly believe it was one of the best jobs on television. We dropped in on the best parts of people's lives. Where else would you be taken to 27 countries and be paid for having all those adventures?

Valerie Singleton had the best phrase for it - she said the job took us 'beyond the rope', the analogy being with the ropes that cordon off the private areas in stately homes. I think that says it all.

But presenting wasn't easy - in all the time I was presenting *Blue Peter* we never used Autocue at all! We had to learn the script and deliver it as accurately as if it was a play. And we had to learn it overnight – my script for the Thursday programme arrived at my house at about 9pm on the Wednesday. Not easy!"

I did my share of the stunts. I made the Rock Climbing and Air Sea Rescue films. I also filmed Jousting, Stunt Cars, Speedway, Trials Riding and American Grid-Iron Football - there really is a long list of very exciting films. And if you weren't impressed with my walking the suspension cable of the Forth Road Bridge, then I give up!

The three of us got on very well indeed. Obviously over ten and a half years of working under that kind of pressure there were times when we would argue – it would be extraordinary if we had not! I can remember one occasion in Mexico when Val and I fell out over something – I can't recall what – and for three days we only spoke to each other through John.

I am still in contact with John and Valerie, though I have lost touch with Lesley over the past ten years."

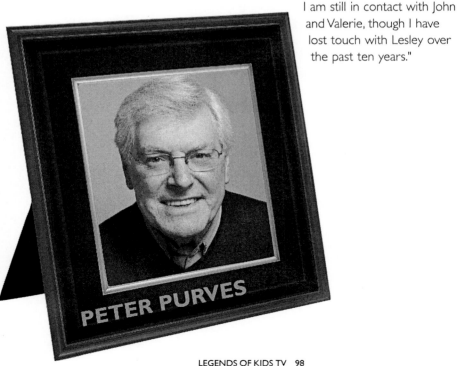

PETER PURVES

MICK ROBERTSON
MAGPIE, FREETIME

Growing up in the 1970s it would be fair to say there was a passing resemblance between glam rock star Marc Bolan and TV presenter Mick Robertson – the dashing good looks and the curly mop top, but fortunately for the TV lovers Mick didn't wrap himself round a tree in an unfortunate motoring accident!

Mick was permanent fixture on our screens for much of the 70s and 80s and even though he is now behind the scenes, he's still working his magic for todays generation of children.

"I had previously trained to be a teacher at Goldsmiths University and always had an interest in working with kids, but teaching is a hard job and on leaving university I met someone in TV and went straight into a job at Rediffusion Television as a runner. It was easier in those days, back in the 70s. I was discovered working behind the scenes, and I went on to work on David Jacob's show *Words & Music* looking after guests. I then went on to be the lowly researcher on a programme called *Come Here Often* a kids show presented by Sarah Ward and the former Welsh rugby star Cliff Morgan. They needed someone to present their talent show segment and I was manoevered in front of the camera and my presenting career grew from that.

Eventually Rediffusion lost its contract and the programme finished and I went back to being a researcher with Thames TV and I was having a nice time in London behind the scenes, helping to create *Magpie* initially. Tony Bastable who was presenting the show moved on, and I auditioned to be the presenter and I got the job. It was my first time presenting regularly and I went on to present it for 10 years! It was a terrific time, a very happy *and* lucky time. It was a job that allowed me to do

everything and live out fantasies. There was a huge variety of activities that kids would love to have a go at and there wasn't a better job doing that on TV.

During that time I tried to keep in touch with the people I was presenting to as I didn't want to lose touch with who they are and never wanted to patronise the audience. I felt connected with ordinary kids because I felt I was ordinary. The Education Act, brought in after World War 2, created opportunities for ordinary people to take priveleged jobs and kids had the chance to do amazing things. I had a humble background but got into a lovely position. It was a very 60s thing and it brought in a new energy. It was a priveleged decade to become an adult.

Magpie fought the battle for ITV for kids but we outlived our time. If I was the producer I would have moved myself on — new blood was needed to be injected, new faces, like *Blue Peter* did. *Magpie* never built up a brand, which is essential for a long running show. Flagship programmes are vital and those who ended its run would admit it was the wrong decision, and there then followed a decline on ITV of kids programming.

After *Magpie* I carried on presenting with other shows, notably *Freetime* which ran for a few years, then I went into satellite TV programming. I felt I was getting too old for presenting and wanted to turn my hand to creating programmes. I'd had a wonderful, fun time.

I went on to establish *The Children's Channel* in 1984, it was a new concept at the time, a dedicated kids channel and the first on the block. Now there is CBBC, Nickelodeon etc. The viewing numbers for satellite TV wasn't a lot then, and the channel gradually declined.

I went on to produce *Wise Up* on Channel 4 which ran for 10 years and was immensely successful, winning 3 International Emmys in 3 years which was a unique achievement and one of my proudest moments. I also developed *Nick News* which was a news show for kids, something more child-friendly than *Newsround*, but it was too expensive to be made weekly.

Another notable achievement was when we won the Japan prize for a programme we had made about Jamaica. It's a world TV award and very rare for people in the UK to win it.

I'm still creating TV shows for Channel 5 and Nickelodeon and enjoying it immensely."

In 2007 Mick was awarded a Special Award Children's BAFTA for his work in television. On receiving his award he said: "I am hugely proud to be receiving my BAFTA award. My television career has been entirely spent in making programmes for children. There is no more important audience. All my programmes have been in the factual entertainment genre which is fast disappearing from children's screens because of its minority appeal. I hope ways will be found to support factual television for children in the future. They should always enjoy a rich and varied viewing choice."

ROD, JANE AND FREDDY
RAINBOW, ROD JANE & FREDDY

Rod, Jane and Freddy are one of those famous trios that everyone seems to know. Shake, Rattle & Roll – Earth, Wind & Fire – Curly, Larry & Mo – Bacon, Lettuce & Tomato... but unlike the others, Rod Jane and Freddy are synonymous with kids TV having entertained and educated a generation of children, and tonight, for your delictation, all three of them are here in one fun bundle, brought to you by the woman who put the 'Jane' into Rod, Jane & Freddy – the one and only Jane Tucker.

"Before I painted the whole world with a rainbow I was a young actress working for BBC Radio playing little boys! I began my career at the age of 3, studying to be a concert pianist and wanting to be a ballerina, but soon realised it was an actor's life for me!

I studied at the Guildhall School of Music and Drama in London. After graduating I followed the classic route of repertory theatre, touring, small parts on TV and regular work on BBC Radio, where my 'little boys voices' were my speciality!

I lived in the same town as Rod in Buckinghamshire at the time, Rod and I had known each other since childhood and our lives went along in parallel lines.

Rod studied art at City and Guilds of London Art School and the London College of Printing.

He became an illustrator and designer for some very famous publishing companies creating some marvellous book covers, and famous logos. But he had lost interest in the design industry and hankered after something more creative, he loved music and wanted to write songs. So he gave up the 9 to 5 and set off busking all over Europe for 2 years! He was a great banjo player and an excellent songwriter.

Rod and I got married after that and we formed a little band called 'Cumulus,' with our best friend Iain Patterson (aka Lofty!)

We played in pubs and clubs and the odd wedding or party. We were essentially a folk group I suppose, but mostly we sang Rod's material. He had written some beautiful songs with fabulous lyrics. He taught me everything I know about writing a song.

Rod played banjo, Lofty played guitar and I played keyboards. We appeared on the talent show *Opportunity Knocks* and won in the studio but we were up against an Irish ballad singer called Joe Cuddy who just pipped us at the post!

The audition for *Rainbow* came shortly after this. My agent had told me to have a children's song ready, so Rod wrote me a special song called 'Great Big Grey Elephants'. It was a delightful song which we've sung many times on the show since.

The creator and producer of *Rainbow* was Pamela Lonsdale. I did a very good audition and she obviously liked me and said she was actually looking for 3 singers/musicians. Well, Pamela was a very generous natured lady, and when I told her that Rod was outside waiting for me she immediately said, 'Oh, bring him in!' So Rod, who had brought his banjo (just in case!), sat down with me and we rattled off a few more numbers. You could see the delight on Pam's face. When we'd finished she took us up to her office where she handed us 2 Rainbow badges and said 'Welcome to Rainbow'! We were over the moon!

We started *Rainbow* in September 1974 alongside Matthew Corbett, who had auditioned separately, ironically with Freddy! – Freddy's audition No. 1 for the show! We were known as Rod Matt and Jane. We had a lot of songwriting and recording to do, but in those days we kept the arrangements fairly simple.

Matthew left after 2 years, he had to take over *Sooty* because his dad, Harry, had a heart attack.

The auditions for Matthew's replacement were farcical! Our head of department had her own ideas about who should be our next musical partner which wasn't quite what we had in mind! Enter Freddy again – audition No.2! He was just what we were looking for but unfortunately it wasn't to be this time. But because of an equity ruling, the newly appointed *Rainbow* recruit was axed and it was back to the drawing board with a new set of auditions. This time Roger Walker got the job and he stayed with us for 3 years.

By the time Roger left we had a new head of department, so I called Freddy who was in between acting jobs and told him to get ready for another audition for Rainbow. He was rather sceptical about going through all that again but I promised him it would be third time lucky. And it was!

Freddy trained at Central School of Speech and Drama. After graduating he spent the next nine years working in various repertory theatres throughout the country playing everything from Shakespeare to musical theatre.

In London's West End he performed at the Royal Court and The Duke of Yorks in *Life Class*, and played Brad in *The Rocky Horror Show* at the Kings Road Theatre and the Comedy Theatre.

His television credits include: *Z Cars*, *The Sweeney*, *The Professionals*, *Horizon*, *Churchill's People*, plus endless TV appearances in commercials.

He'd just finished making an advert for Galaxy chocolate prior to being finally offered the job on Thames Television's now famous kids show *Rainbow*.

Incidentally, something that not many people know about is that at one point in the late seventies, Freddy, Matthew Corbett and Geoffrey Hayes were all in rep. together in Dundee before going their separate ways! Spooky that!

So Freddy's audition No. 3 really was third time lucky! Rod and I were thrilled to have him aboard and at last, in 1980, *Rod Jane and Freddy* was born!

By now our schedule was phenomenal! With the arrival of Freddy our musical arrangements were becoming fairly complex, so our work load was tremendous.

In a nutshell, our schedule consisted of writing songs for the 'Theme of the Day' on Rainbow. With 3 shows a week, that meant 9 songs on the go: 3 being written, 3 being recorded, and 3 being performed by us at Thames Television Studios. Freddy played guitars and bass, Rod played drums and I played keyboards.

Monday night we would record three songs plus any incidental music in the sound studio at Thames, after rehearsing all day in the Yacht club at Teddington Lock. Tuesday we had more rehearsals and a Producer's run. Wednesday we were in Studio 3 recording 2 whole shows. Thursday was another day in the studio recording one show only. Everybody except us had the rest of the week and the weekend off! Friday/Saturday/Sunday we would be arranging the next week's songs for the following week! What a schedule!!!

A lot of hard work but come the studio days it was fun, fun, fun all the way with George, Zippy, Bungle and Geoffrey. We laughed our way through 1000 *Rainbows* and more.

We'd often be in stitches and there was an enormous amount of innuendo. In those days we had what is known as a 'dress rehearsal' before the final 'take', and this is where we got away with murder! There was one time when Bungle (played by Stanley Bates) had been shopping and had a basket full of props. He'd read out his list: butter, eggs, bread etc and pulled them out of the basket one by one, but in the dress rehearsal the props in the basket had changed to a vibrator, whip, mask, crotchless knickers...

There was another time when we were all going for a picnic, and Bungle had on his big khaki shorts. He layed out the picnic, bent over with his enormous bottom to the camera and said "Ohh, what an enormous spread!"

Within a year of Freddy joining we were given our own show. This came about when there was a spare slot in the programme schedules. A science programme called *Spectrum* had been dropped through lack of viewing figures. Charles Warren, our producer, offered it to us. He thought we could sit on three stools and sing old Rainbow songs and be called 'Rhondo' or 'Allegro'! We, of course, thought differently! Spare slots don't come along that often, this was our chance to be creative, and together with director John Woods we came up with a series of musical stories with wonderful characters and fantastic situations ranging from 'Fairies and Goblins' at the bottom of the garden to 'germs' down a plughole, to 'Little Miss Muffet' meets 'Spaceman Zoom'!

As to the title of the show it was decided it would be called simply *Rod Jane and Freddy*, and would run 13 minutes per episode. These shows had very elaborate costumes and make up, but no scenery!

The first 4 series involved a whole new concept in television programming using a technique called Ultimatte. This technique electronically placed us onto a caption that gave us a background to work in i.e. in a drawing of an alley way we were superimposed as 'cats'!

For these shows we won an award in America for Technical Merit, being quite 'cutting edge' at the time.

We did 7 series in all, changing the format from series 5 onwards to our now familiar black and white look on stage. These shows were based more on using your imagination with songs and sketches, dance and mime, utilising the minimum of costumes and creating sets and situations with inventive props. A much more simple approach but very creative and gave us an identity.

This show transferred perfectly to the real stage and in 1990 when Thames TV lost its franchise, we took our *Rod Jane & Freddy Show* and set off on a

ROD, JANE
AND FREDDY

Nationwide tour and played every major theatre in Great Britain and Northern Ireland. 2 tours a year for 6 years! Brilliant! Hard work and a hectic life, but we loved being in front of live audiences after all those years on TV.

In 1996 we won the BACS (British Academy of Composers and Songwriters) Gold Badge Award for outstanding contribution to the music industry. A gift from our peers for writing some 2000 songs spanning 22 years, this had to be the pinnacle of our careers, and in the autumn of that year we decided to call it a day.

We did our final show in Tunbridge Wells to a full house. We were showered with flowers and gifts and it felt very emotional, we'd had a long run.

I think *Rainbow* worked because we cared about what we were doing. We were all actors with strong emotions and the 'Magic 7' just gelled so well, and *Rod, Jane & Freddy* had a culty charm to it. These days it's all about money. Merchandising first, then the programme. There was a time when the Rainbow puppets weren't even copyright protected. It wasn't until Bobby Davro came to guest and brought in his own giants puppets of Zippy and George that the producers realised there was no protection and they quickly had them copywritten.

Since then we've performed together in Pantomime and various TV shows including Peter Kay's music video with the Proclaimers, and several RJF personal appearances on Sky.

Freddy's written scripts for *Sooty* and *Playdays*, we've written the music for *Wizadora, Playdays* and songs for pantomimes. The last RJF panto was in 2004.

We've been incredibly lucky and had the most fascinating, fantastic and fabulous careers.

Since then the boys have opted to have a different life for a change. They both have things they want to do outside the business and a bit of just living really!

As for me, I'm writing a ballet. The dream remains, only I won't be in it. But I'm still treading the boards in Panto every year, playing the Good Fairy and dancing around the stage waving my magic wand, some things will never change!"

ALAN ROTHWELL
PICTURE BOX, HICKORY HOUSE

It wasn't until I saw the titles on YouTube that it struck me how much I loved Hickory House. One of those gems that had floated to the deepest recess of my memory. It must be 30 years since I'd heard the theme tune, and it made the hairs on the back of my neck stand on end. Alan was not only a resident of Hickory House alongside Dusty and Humphrey, but also the genial host of the long running film show Picture Box, complete with its haunting yet intriguing theme. But before all that, Alan was a resident at another famous location...

"I'd been on *Coronation Street* for 8 years playing David Barlow and when that role finished in 1968 Granada were looking for someone to present *Picture Box*. There were 3 of us in the running to get the job, one of the others being George Best. Considering his subsequent lifestyle, I think the producers were quite glad they didn't choose him.

I went on to present it for 18 years from 1968-86 and it became well known to a whole generation of young people. The theme music was very curious, with a haunting quality. It was played on a glass harmonica. Occasionally, some people have said to me, 'I used to hate Picture Box.' When asked why, they would always say it was because they found the music was scary. But on the whole, it was an extremely well-loved show. It was produced by John Coop who was a lovely gentle man, who made lovely gentle programmes. The whole idea of the show was to introduce films from all over the world; Hungary, Russia, China, Canada, Japan to school children. They were really excellent films that would never have been seen otherwise.

One of the most famous ones was *The Red Balloon*, a French film about a little boy who finds a red balloon which begins to follow him to school. It was live action, but you could see the balloon being tugged by a string. The balloon became the boy's little friend and he would get into trouble with a group of bad kids, and the balloon would help get him out of trouble, until one day, one of the bad kids threw a brick at the balloon, and the balloon slowly deflated. It took about thirty seconds to die. It was incredibly moving, and all the kids as well as the teachers watching would be in tears. It ended happily, however. All the balloons in the town gathered around the boy who took hold of their strings, and was lifted high into the sky.

One other film the kids loved was called *Nahanny*, a true story about an old man who lived in a log cabin in Canada by the Nahanny river. Once a year, in the summer, he would build a boat to travel up the river's rapids on a search for gold. At one point he had to leave the river and carry the boat's engine and all his equipment up past a particularly nasty stretch, then build another boat to continue his journey. He did this for 25 years, and as far as we know he never found any gold. This epic annual journey fascinated our viewers, who often wrote to ask him if he had ever been successful. Sadly I don't think he ever received their letters for they were never answered.

When *Picture Box* began, TV was still in black and white and the films, some of which were in gorgeous Technicolour, could only be seen in boring monochrome, so we had a *Picture Box Roadshow*. We chose the best-loved and most beautiful films and took them round the country, showing them on big cinema screens, as they were meant to be seen. The idea was wonderfully successful. School parties came out from schools in their thousands to see it, and we even managed to fill the 3,000 seater Apollo cinema in Manchester – twice! *Picture Box* was aimed at 9-13 year olds but there were also some tiny tots came and great 16 and 17 year olds turned up who were a lot bigger than me!

Towards the end of *Picture Box*'s run, John Coop had left Granada, and I wrote and produced the show and chose the films. It became my baby, and something I am now, looking back, most proud of.

Picture Box was full of excellent teaching resources, with booklets attached to it for teachers and that's (one of the reasons) why it was so successful. The show was created by Sybil Marshall. Sybil had previously written a highly influential book called *Experiments in Education*, and she wrote all the booklets that to accompanied the programme. We would get lots of letters, and teachers in particular would say, 'What would we do without it'. We were also told about one gang of kids who, after a

ALAN OUTISDE HICKORY HOUSE

programme on the white rhinoceros, built one in their class-room to scale. Pictures of it got into the National press but the rhino itself never saw the light of day. It was too big to get out of the room.

When *Picture Box* finished two things happened. The main TV companies had to outsource some programmes for other companies to make so there was more diversity, and Granada decided which ones to keep and which to let go. They held onto *Coronation Street* and *World in Action* tightly but *Picture Box* was one that they let go together with all their other schools programmes.

It was given to Eddie Shah who was starting a TV company. Eddie used to be Floor Manager on *Coronation Street*, and I first met him when we played poker in the dressing room. We didn't really play for serious money, but we played for enough to get excited about it. The thinking behind the shows creation had changed and it was decided that there wasn't enough going on in schools about teaching children to read and write. *Picture Box* was regarded as being a bit too adventurous. I saw the point at the time and accepted it. It had run its course.

Hickory House was also produced by John Coop. It was quite a heavy workload as there were just the two of us presenting the show, with of course, the puppeteer. I worked with Amanda Barrie, Julia North and Louise Hall-Taylor in my 5 years on the show. We would record 5 shows in a week which was an hour and a quarter of TV time, whereas *The Street*, say, was only 2 shows a week and had a cast of around 25 actors at a time in the episodes. So no, Hickory House was not an easy show to work on.

It was really interesting working with puppets, though. Barry Smith was behind Dusty Mop and Humphrey Cushion, whose voice was very similar to Barry's normal voice. Poor Barry spent most of the time under the sofa and had only a camera to see what was going on. But the image he saw on his monitor was opposite to the way he had to move, so he had to work out a way of doing it. Barry was also a voice coach, and one of his clients was Laurence Olivier. It was at the time Olivier was playing *Othello* and wanted a deeper and more resonant voice. Barry would take pleasure in coming in and saying, "Guess who I had as a pupil, yesterday..."

I filmed 60 episodes in total, and it was a great time. There was one occasion I had to be Wee Willie Winkie, dressed in a long nightie and carrying a candle, and I couldn't do it for laughing. I had to peep round a big box at the camera and start reciting the poem, but I started to laugh, and then the cameraman caught the bug, and the times when I kept a straight face, he would start laughing so it took us absolutely ages before we got the take.

I was working in the theatre whilst doing the TV work, as it wasn't a full time job, The theatre has always been my special love. It's where I first started at the age of eleven. I don't do so much acting these days. Every now and again someone needs an old geezer and I pop up from time to time – I was in an episode of *Shameless* just recently.

I often turn my hand to directing these days. I've just directed a play in a Manchester festival. Six short plays in one evening, all written by TV writers for shows like *Coronation Street* and *Emmerdale*. It ran for a fortnight. I've got another play coming up to direct, and I'm also looking to publish a book I've written called *Higher than the Hawk – The Atheists' Guide to the Afterlife*, so I keep myself pretty busy.

It's always great to hear people who remember the TV programmes so fondly. Some things stick with you as you get older. As a kid I remember how I loved *Children's Hour* on the radio, and the music, and the programmes and the characters are still here with me now. It's nice to know I'm part of fond memories in other people's minds."

PAT SHARP
FUN HOUSE, WHAT'S UP DOC?

Pat Sharp dominated children's telly as host of the extremely popular *Fun House*. Accompanied by the twins, Melanie and Martina, he made sure he put the fun into Fun House - action packed and messy, and sporting a just as legendary hairdo! All hail Mr. Fun House.

"Before (and after) *Fun House* I was (and am still) a radio presenter. It's what I've always done. In 1982 I started off on Radio 1, sitting in for Steve Wright. I went on to spend 10 years at Capital Radio following Chris Tarrant at Breakfast, after which I moved to Heart, where I remain to this day.

As a child I used to watch the filming of the sitcom *The Good Life* with Richard Briers. This was because it was actually shot at my mate's house near London.

I auditioned for *Fun House* along with John Leslie, just as well I got it as the twins were quite small and John is very tall indeed, the girls would have needed ladders!

The rest is history! After 10 years it was continually top of the ratings. It would regularly get millions of viewers in a time when there weren't 500 channels to choose from, just four.

Each series was shot in just 7 days in Glasgow, filming 2 shows a day, although it seemed I was on TV for a longer time as they were aired weekly. When I met the kids the night before filming they would be outgoing and teasing me about my hair and so on, but when they got in front of the camera they could freeze sometimes.
There was an American version of the show, presented by J D Roth, and the kids were more open on this show.

It developed a real cult status. There are dozens of *Fun House* Facebook groups and internet fan pages these days. Just Google it sometime to see what I mean.

I still get great big muscle bound 6'3" guys coming up to me in the street saying 'You are a legend. You made my childhood. I f*cking love you Pat Sharp.' I've also been called 'Mr Fun House' out of a bus window on many occasions!

Then there was *What's Up Doc?* up against the likes of *Going Live* and *Live & Kicking* which became the first ITV Saturday morning kids show to beat the BBC for viewing figures. I hosted this too with Andy Crane and Yvette Fielding for 3 years.

There were some great times on *Fun House*, and lots of funny moments. There was a time when one of the go-karts failed to stop. I'd waved the flag but it kept on going and smacked into me. I was in so much pain but had to carry on!

There was one evening in, after filming, when I left the hotel with the twins, Melanie and Martina, to go out for a meal and we came across a drunk in the Glasgow streets. He staggered up to me and said 'You're that moron, aren't you', I said 'If you say so!', 'Are those the twins?', 'Yeah.' 'How old are they?', '22', 'What? Each??!' and he wandered off!"

Fun House has recently returned to our screens on Challenge TV where they are re-running the old shows for a whole new audience.

PAT SHARP

GAY SOPER
THE FLUMPS

Posie, Perkin and Pootle, those loveable, animated balls of fluff that were the Flumps. They were so furry and cute, how could you not like the Flumps? Who could forget Pootle inflating his balloon by sticking it in the end of Grandpa's Flumpet!? Created by Julie Holder and brought to life by the talent of Gay Soper, who not only narrated the series but performed all the voices with such aplomb.

"I became the voice of The Flumps because my agent, April Young, suggested me to David Yates, the producer of the series. He had asked her if June Whitfield, one of April's clients, could do the job, but June wasn't free and April suggested me. I was a very experienced voice over artist who had made many a radio and TV commercial, using a wide range of accents, styles of speaking, characters and vocal tones.

I went to see David and auditioned. We tried out several accents – my own accent is what I would call Standard English, or 'Received Pronunciation' (I always think that is a stupidly affected phrase) – and in those days, Standard English was regarded as practically politically incorrect. So a regional accent was requested. As far away from the Home Counties as possible!! We tried a couple of different Scottish accents, a little bit of Welsh, a West Country accent, a Liverpool accent, and we ended up with what became the accent of the Flumps, a sort of fairly generalised Midlands-to-Yorkshire accent. Probably a little bland but it seemed to do the trick. I got the job. I don't remember receiving any advice about working in Childrens TV, but it was all a lot of fun.

Apart from being a busy voice over artist, I was well known for my leading roles in West End musicals including Canterbury Tales, the original West End cast of Godspell, and the role of Barbara opposite Michael Crawford in Billy at Drury Lane, and many more. I was also known for several sit-coms on the TV including Susan Crichton Jones in Romany Jones with

POOTLE

Arthur Mullard and Queenie Watts; and episodes of series such as *Father Dear Father* and *Bless This House* with Sid James and others.

After *The Flumps* I was, and still am, in West End productions – I was Madame Thenardier for three years in *Les Miserables* at the Palace Theatre from 1988 - 1991, I was in the Olivier Award winning production of *Sunday In The Park With George*, and most recently *Marguerite* at the Theatre Royal Haymarket, the latest musical written by Bloublil and Shoenberg, who wrote *Les Miserables*. Further TV appearances included playing opposite John Wells in two series of *Rude Health* on Channel 4.

My own childhood favourites were *Popeye, Bill and Ben, Andy Pandy* and *Listen With Mother* on the Radio.

I hope this book will help to raise funds to help those children less fortunate than us, and in the hope that there may always be wonderful programmes for children to watch and listen to, to feed their imaginations with colour and fill their hearts full of joy and a little magic."

Gay has a solo cabaret act and recently produced her first solo album, which is available at Dress Circle www.dresscircle.co.uk

GAY SOPER

NICK SPARGO
WILLO THE WISP

In 1981 BBC began airing the first series of *Willo the Wisp* to a teatime audience just before the early evening news on BBC1. The audience figures for the children's animation series averaged nine million, which has never been surpassed. Nick Spargo's wonderful animation, brought to life by Kenneth Williams' wickedly voiced creatures living deep in Doyley Woods, became ingrained in a generation's psyche.

Nick's eldest daughter Bobbie worked as a character designer and animator with her father in the 1970's and was went on to be a successful illustrator of children's books, producing over 30 books with major publishing houses. She talks about her fathers work and Willo's 2005 return.

"Having seen the success of the *Mr. Men* my father wanted to come up with a show about a group of characters that had merchandising potential. The environment, Doyley Woods surrounded our then home outside Henley-on-Thames in Oxfordshire. Moog the dog certainly reflected the character of our rather daft labrador dog.

I never met Kenneth Williams and my father only knew him professionally. He would come into the recording studio and do the whole thing in one take.

It was a lot of hard work bringing *Willo the Wisp* back in 2005! Brilliantly voiced by James Dreyfus, it took 5 years from start to completion. The actual production took 9 months, but the other year was spent trying to get a broadcaster, actor, money and team together.

We don't have any animations planned at the moment. Animation is very much in the doldrums in the UK with BBC budgets being cut, no advertising revenues to put into broadcasting resulting in CITV closing down, and what work we have, being done abroad in India where labour is cheap.

I am quite old, so my favourite kids programmes were *Andy Pandy* and *Bill and Ben* – first time round, but I liked *Noggin the Nog* best."

You can relive all your *Willo the Wisp* memories at www.willothewisp.co.uk

ED STEWART
CRACKERJACK

It's Friday, five-to-five... or was it? Prior to his stint on *Crackerjack* Ed was one of the first DJs to join Radio 1 in 1967 and has had a long, successful career on the airwaves since. Ed reveals some secrets of *Crackerjack's* filming and being the ever generous man, he even bought me a pint when we met!

"When I was presenting *Junior Choice* on Radio 1 in 1968 there wasn't much TV. Radio was the only thing people had. Michael Aspel was so popular presenting *Family Fun* getting 25 million listeners and I was getting 16 million.

I'd previously started on pirate radio but the Government closed down the station because they thought they were illegal.

Music was governed by the Musician's Union and it was costly to play songs on the BBC with very few shows having 100% 'needle time' (needle time being the amount of time playing music) and the BBC thought we didn't pay anything, but we did pay something.

My agent was approached, knowing that I was popular with kids and they thought I'd be the right person to take over from Michael Aspel.

It was only when Noel Edmonds transferred to TV that he made it popular.

I went on to present the *Way Out Show* in 1967 and *Ed and Zed*, and also a programme called *Stewpot* on ITV which was cancelled. I'd signed a 26 week contract which got paid in full after just 2 weeks!

Rupert Murdoch took over LWT and he wanted 'tits and bums' and no kids stuff. *The Roger Whittaker Show* had dancing girls and it was going out at 5.30-6.15 in the evening.

I presented *Top of the Pops* in the 70s. I was mainly a stand-in presenter. I always preferred radio really. George Martin once said "Radio's the mother of TV, and they're still looking for the father!"

Crackerjack was filmed in a theatre at the BBC. It looked manic on screen but that was down to the editing as the filming was quite stop/start if the lights were not in the right place and so on. It was actually recorded on a Thursday. The cock-ups were left in so it had the appearance of being live. I would be driving home on a Friday and there would be 20 different TV shows all playing *Crackerjack* in Radio Rental's shop window. I couldn't stop and be noticed otherwise it would break the illusion of being live.

I worked with Peter Glaze who was a great man. He was a vaudeville actor and understudy to The Crazy Gang. But the producer of Crackerjack wanted to change the presenters and brought in The Krankies, but I made the decision for them.

In about 1979 or 80 I moved from Radio 1 to Radio 2 and presented *Family Favourites*. I worked on Radio Mercury until 1990 and in 1991, I was invited back to Radio 2 by the new controller.

About 5 years ago I worked for a radio station in Spain for about 6 months. They have since invited me back, but my priorities have changed since then.

I did try to get a job on Classic FM. I come from a classical family and I'm a classically trained musician. They asked me to send my CV, then they asked what my name was again! So that was the end of that!

I've also worked with the late artist and presenter Mark Speight in panto. He drew a caricature of me as a gift, but it was such a tragedy. He was a very talented artist.

As a kid, TV hardly existed but we did have radio. I especially enjoyed listening to *Dick Barton Special Agent*. Charles Williams wrote the theme music 'The Devil's Gallop' and also 'The Dream of Olwen'. He wrote for Chappells as their in-house composer so he didn't get any royalties, just his £25 a week wage.

Looking back I'm proud of the transition from pirate radio to Radio 1. Good fortune and timing were on my side at that time. Presenting *Junior Choice* for 12 years was another highlight. At first only the producer's wife heard it, and they were so slow in offering me a contract. They kept asking me if I could come back next week. This went on for 6 months before they finally gave me a 3 month contract. It was such a relief!"

CRACKERJACK

CHRIS TARRANT
TISWAS

Saturdays are *still* TISWAS days in my opinion, even after 27 years having passed since the last show was transmitted. This chaotic and anarchic world which included the likes of Trevor McDougnut, Houdi Elbow, the Phantom Flan Flinger, custard pies and lots of buckets of water was integral to my viewing, and not forgetting Chris' co-host, the alluring Sally James. This game-show king will soon be coming back to kids TV. This is what we want!

"My first TV job was as a reporter on the nightly six o'clock news show in Birmingham for ATV. I did that for a couple of years and then a guy called Peter Harris, who went on to direct *The Muppets*, rang me out of the blue and said would I be interested in presenting a new show they were trying for kids on Saturday morning. It was to be an extra £25 a week for 3 hours. I jumped at the chance! What I didn't realise was that the thing was to take over my life for the next 7 years and become a huge national cult!

In those early days in 1974 there was no real television audience on any of the stations on Saturday morning. Several of them didn't open at all until midday, some of them just ran wall to wall cartoons or very old black and white films... but once *TISWAS* came onto the scene it was the end of all that. It was also the end of Saturday morning pictures. Parents no longer needed to slog into town to sit with their kids watching ancient Hopalong Cassidy films when they could carry on doing the housework with the kids at home in front of the telly.

TISWAS was an instant success, at first locally in the Midlands TV area, and then nationally. A couple of years later the BBC introduced the *Multi-Coloured Swap Shop* with Noel Edmonds as they too had now realised there was a serious audience out there to be won on a Saturday morning. *TISWAS* was still probably the best fun I've ever had during my career. We literally lived, slept and ate it every week... and smelt of custard all the time for seven years! We also became great mates. We spent so long together writing and presenting the show, and then the extraordinary chaotic tours after the series was over, that we became a huge part of each other's lives.

We all still see a lot of each other, as if nothing's changed. We carry on conversations as if we'd seen each other five minutes before... but then we have known each other for nearly 30 years. Ouch!!

Since then, I've gone on to do all sorts of things. The big change in my life was discovering the joys of radio in 1984. I love the liveness of it, I love the spontaneity of it and I've been doing it at Capital Radio for 17 years and now at Smooth Radio. I also present a little show called *Who Wants to be a Millionaire* that seems to have been quite popular and is now going out in 120 countries around the world!

The best piece of career advice I've ever received is probably just 'Be yourself'. And I think I more or less always have been.

I've never really had many favourite kids TV programmes. To be truthful, I was never a great fan of kids television but then again I never really thought of *TISWAS* as a kids show. When we used to do the tours it was written on the ticket – no person UNDER the age of 16 is allowed in this auditorium. At one point, 53 % of the audience of *TISWAS* were discovered to be over 18! It worked on two levels and was very much an adult and student cult.

However, I do remember watching *Bill & Ben* very avidly as a tiny little boy and I used to love *The Clangers*."

Chris is returning to kids TV with *Tarrant Lets The Kids Loose* on Watch, which will give three to six-year-olds a go at fulfilling their ambitions in the adult world. Chris said "This show totally captures the spirit and the inherent comedy of children – it's the kind of family entertainment I love."

CHRIS TARRANT

RICHARD VOBES
SNUG & COZI

During the 1990s a pair of comedy aliens landed from the planet Squadge, and onto CITV – characters somewhat akin to an outer space Laurel & Hardy! But Richard's experiences with the TV executives highlights a stark contrast in programme production values compared with the shows made back in the 70s. Richard is now an award winning and prolific internet podcaster – from a beach hut in Worthing!

"Prior to the birth of Snug and Cozi I was doing a number of different things, from entertaining at corporates events, festivals and gala days which included mime, robotics, juggling, lying on beds of nails and walking on glass, to name but a few.

I was on my way to a gig when I saw a shop called 'Snug and Cosy Bedroom Furniture' and I thought what a great name for a kids programme. I had been writing loads of children's programmes in my earlier life and submitting them to TV companies and getting the usual rejection letters. This time I thought instead of writing just a script and sending it off I thought why not actually make a pilot episode in film. I also, as a kid, had been experimenting with film making.

As I thought about the idea and the strange title, an idea start to brew in my mind about two crazy spacemen who crash land on the Earth and all the adventures they could have. It's not a unique idea, but working with a friend of mine, also in the business, it could be very different. I always likened it to Laurel and Hardy in spacesuits and of course slapstick humour never goes out of fashion with kids.

I gathered a crew together and we shot a pilot episode of this programme on

16mm film. The two idiotic spacemen, in the pilot, take their names from crash landing into a furniture store with the same name as I saw on my gig. In fact I had the signage above the shop fall onto their heads adjacent to the respective names to make it abundantly clear.

The show was eventually sold to Scottish Television, who promised us the world, but unfortunately delivered little, going back on their words when it came to the signing the final contract. I remember pointing out all the additional points we had agreed on that they had left out with the then executive producer who simply turned round and said, 'Do you want to be on television or not?'

So we had no choice but to except their terms and we started to film. The experience of the two directors who were assigned to us were very limited when it came to children's television and the final programming was never as good as I would have liked. As performers we were prepared to do crazy stunts, to enhance the quality of kids programmes on TV, but the producers treated the show as a non entity with little importance. It was important to us. It was our careers. We did manage to get one stunt that was in the original script and wasn't dumbed down, that of Snug and Cozi riding in a double bed out of control down a hill and ending up in a car wash and covered in foam. I wanted Snug to get wrapped round the big roller - but they weren't having that!

It was after that experience with larger TV companies that I vowed I would only work with smaller independent companies where I could have more say in how the comedy was developed. Comedy is a craft and cannot be directed by accountants. It is very rare indeed to find any good British made comedy in the current television industry, unfortunately.

When we were on television the doors were open to me to pitch many ideas, but as soon as our series was finished the TV executives shut those doors. I pitched ideas many times and although many commissioning executives complimented me on the video pilots I was producing they still turned down the projects as it seemed we were not in with old school tie network and after a while I looked to the internet as a means of getting my products to the audience without the middleman. The copyright of the characters are mine now and if I could find a way to fund the show again I would do it like a shot!"

From a beach hut in Worthing, West Sussex, you can hear the daily 'Vobes Show' and check out the Vobes blog at www.vobes.com

ROGER WALKER
RAINBOW

I always had an affection for Roger Walker in *Rainbow* – jolly, friendly and cuddly – just like me as a child (but without the moustache). He accompanied Rod and Jane after the Sooty-bound Matthew Corbett and before the incoming Freddie. Roger talks about his time on *Rainbow*, his later career and about playing with his twanger!

"It was by chance that *Rainbow* came about. First and foremost I never considered myself as a real musician. I could play a bit of guitar, banjo, keyboards and harmonica, but I was just a jobbing actor from the Potteries who had come to do a play in London when I got a call from Liz Sadler, who was the casting director at Thames TV. She was looking for someone in their early thirties for a 'general' casting, which was then used as an introduction and as a get together with Rod and Jane. Matthew Corbett was already on *Rainbow*, but his father Harry had a heart attack, and Matthew took over working with Sooty as well as doing *Rainbow*, and when Matthew went full time with Sooty, they needed a replacement. Urgently.

It was a matter of being in the right place at the right time. I had the casting on the Tuesday and I got the job on the Friday. But it was a baptism of fire. We had to write, record and perform 3 songs a week as well as creating nursery rhymes and it really was working 25 hours a day, 8 days a week. In nearly 3 years and 10 series we must have written about 120 songs!

It was a fun time but hard work. There was a good family atmosphere at Thames TV. Matthew Corbett kept up good relations with us after he left and we occasionally guested on *The Sooty Show*.

The infamous "Twangers" video was done one lunch time. It was written by Roy Skelton and Stanley Bates who played Bungle. It was never meant for public viewing but since it appeared on YouTube some 30 years later, it's become a classic clip. It was done at a time when Monty Python and Pete & Dud were popular, and there was always competition between the engineers at Thames TV and the BBC to produce 'a bit of daftness' for internal consumption at Christmas time.

I eventually wanted to return to mainstream acting and I decided to leave *Rainbow* to follow my acting career. I later worked on *CBTV* which was

another Thames TV children's show, which was a follow-on from *Magpie* fronted by Paul Shearer and Anneka Rice, I played Arnold Buggins who ran the paint shop.

Thames TV were very loyal and I guested on *The Sooty Special*, playing a Brummie Father Christmas with June Whitfield's daughter, Susie Aitchison as my elfin helper. I also worked with Stuart Hall, the director, who was a super fun fellow and a great practical joker.

I've also played the nasty landlord in *The Queen's Nose*, thirty episodes of *Big Deal* as Kipper, and Bunny Charlson in *Eldorado*, but that wasn't a happy experience at all. My story line was not very believable and some scripts were often poor. In the end, I handed in my notice after 6 months, but actually stayed on for another 3 months and contrary to newspaper reports at the time, I was the only actor to resign of his own accord.

Among the highlights of my career, apart from literally dozens of TV appearances, working at The Royal Shakespeare Company, The Haymarket Theatre with Sir Peter Hall and Jessica Lange, and at Chichester with the late Ian Richardson, was appearing in a 35 week tour of *Journey's End*, which took in all of the UK as well as the West End. After 400 performances it still seemed fresh.

Another highlight was playing 'Barry', an ambulance paramedic, in the TV series *Picking up the Pieces*, written by Anita J. Pandolfo. It had great storylines and wonderful depth and reality of characters. A good writer is worth their weight in gold!

I've also done my fair share of work on the radio. I spent 6 months with the BBC repertory company – you can play young and thin, with hair.......on the radio!

These days I'm still acting. In 2008 I was in the new Brideshead film and did a national TV commercial and I'm also writing songs again after a thirty-year break and am putting together a CD.

Making music is a hobby now and occasionally I play banjo in local pubs with a country rock band, The Deputies, and I still sing in Teddington Folk Club.

I also read stories at Teddington library a couple of times a year – Summer and around Christmas. One of the guest story tellers on *Rainbow*, Alan Wheatley, who was a well known movie face in the 1950s – a very upright military fellow was thought to be rather stern but he turned out to be the very opposite – told me that he read stories in libraries. I was really impressed. Years later I was approached by Teddington library. It's a lovely thing to do.

In my career in Childrens' Television, I've always tried to spell things out clearly without being patronising. I've always given 110% effort and energy and tried to be as truthful and as real as possible in everything I've done."

You can hear Roger's latest songs by visiting www.myspace.com/banjorogerwalker where there are songs from his latest mini CD.

 **IN MEMORIUM**

Many extremely creative and talented people who have been instrumental in our upbringing, education and entertainment are, sadly, no longer with us.

Tony Hart was my all time hero. I was in total awe of his ability and upon reading an interview a few months before his death where he mentioned he was unable to use his hands, I found it just as upsetting as his passing.

Please take a moment to remember those who have given so much.

Michael Bentine
The Bumblies, Potty Time

Roy Castle
Record Breakers

Michael & Joanne Cole
*Fingerbobs, Bod, Heads & Tails,
Chock-a-Block, Pigeon Street*

Peter Glaze
Crackerjack

Tony Hart
Vision On, Take Hart, Hart Beat

William Hartnell
Doctor Who

Peter Hawkins
*Bill & Ben, Captain Pugwash, The Family
Ness, The Adventures of Sir Prancelot,
Super Ted, Bleep and Booster, Doctor Who*

Rod Hull
Emu

Caron Keating
Blue Peter

Shari Lewis
Lamb Chop

Annette Mills
Muffin the Mule

Johnny Morris
Animal Magic

Ivan Owen
Basil Brush

Jon Pertwee
Doctor Who, Worzel Gummidge

Oliver Postgate
*Pingwings, Pogles' Wood, Noggin the Nog,
Ivor the Engine, Clangers and Bagpuss,*

John Ryan
Creator – Captain Pugwash

Nick Spargo
Creator - Willo the Wisp

Mark Speight
smArt

Michael Staniforth
Timothy Claypole – Rentaghost

Patrick Troughton
Doctor Who

Molly Weir
Hazel the McWitch - Rentaghost

SUBSCRIBERS
THANK YOU TO ALL

Paul R. Jackson
David Stewart
Catherine Christopher
Iain & Joan Cannell
Karl Orbell
Mark Mowbray
Carly Drage
Ronnie Le Drew
Richard Baker
Alan Rothwell
Peter Barclay
Angus Auden
Paul Miller
Ruth Watters
Lisa Iannelli

Lisa Guerriero
Nic Luker
Lisa Steele
Andrew Evans
Emily Horne
Jenny Hughes
Steve Nottage
Alan Young
Maria Sherriff
Eric Suddaby
Sarah Mayes
Steve Phillips
Dominic Taylor
Mary Watson
Kevin Williams

Paula Mickelson
Henry Walters
Stewart Thompson
Val Derrington
Richard Dickinson
Colin Piper
Billy West
Simon Bradbury
Emily Campbell
Ian Edmondson
Virginia Symmonds
Jimmy Fairbanks
Hugh Adams
Nigel Ibbotson
Victor Grimble

CREDITS

Photo credits unknown except: p6 Lynn News, p20-22 Bob Block, p25-27 Bruce Thomas, p29-31 The Cole Estate, p63-64 Vicky Ireland, p70-71 Garry Vaux, p75 Rick Jones & Valerie Neale, p80 Wilf Lunn, p93 Nigel Plaskitt, p101 Mick Robertson, p106 Peter O'Toole, p121-122 Richard Vobes, p124 Roger Walker

PUBLISHING

Other titles from GJB Publishing
York City Memoirs

To order further copies of Legends of Kids TV you can visit

www.legendsofkidstv.co.uk

or

www.GJBpublishing.co.uk

If you are a subscriber you are always entitled to purchase
additional copies with a 25% discount off the retail price.

For all enquiries you can email
enquiries@legendsofkidstv.co.uk

Who is Victor Grimble?